Celebrating
Advent And Christmas
With Children

by Colleen Rooney

*Food Celebrations
with the Saints for Home and School*

Illustrations by Kathleen Woodburn

CreateSpace Independent Publishing Platform
An Amazon.com Company

ISBN: 1490485325
ISBN 13: 9781490485324

Photograph of Colleen Rooney courtesy of Catherine Findlay

❧ **DEDICATION** ❧

To Katherine Agnes Smith Redmond, my maternal grandmother, and to Mary Olive St. John Rooney, my mother-in-law—you remain inspiring examples of faith, love, and steadfastness.

CONTENTS

*Indicates Easy Recipe

ACKNOWLEDGMENTS

I would like to thank my family and friends who have encouraged me in this project, especially my dear husband, Bob, and my friends, Carol Krieger, Rosemary Sporleder, and Fran Van de Voorde. To my parents, Frances and Alan, who shared their love of Christmas with me, who sent me to Catholic schools where the Sisters shared their love of Christ and Christmas, and who made it possible for me to see Europe with its rich Catholic culture as a young woman. To the many wonderful women who have been models of inspiration: my grandmother, Katherine, who let me dabble in the kitchen as a child; my aunt Maria, who introduced me to Maria von Trapp and opened another door to Catholic culture; my mother in-law, Mary Olive Rooney, whose appreciation for all things Catholic spurred me on; and in a very special way to Evelyn Birge Vitz whose cookbook, *A Continual Feast,* has provided years of inspiration and motivation to me and enjoyment for my family, Thank you! To my children (now grown): Patrick, Thomas, Catherine, and Michael, you brought much joy to my life as we celebrated many feast day traditions; and to my grandchildren, Hannah, Jack, Erik, and Vivian, you inspire me to hand on the traditions, so the next generation might enjoy them, too. A warm thank you goes to Sandra Muñoz who introduced Kathleen O'Malley Woodburn to me. Kathleen's illustrations convey the warmth and charm of celebrating the feasts of Advent and Christmas in the home, parish, and school. A note of thanks goes to Betty Wittman, Marianne Christensen, and Vaughn Treco for their invitations to present Catholic food traditions to their classes. And to Nancy Lutz and Rebecca Rooney whose able editing skills provided many corrections and suggestions that are reflected in this book.

❧ INTRODUCTION ❧

This book is written for mothers, catechists, and teachers who are looking for activities and resources that will bring their families or students closer to the true meaning of Christmas: the celebration of the birth of Jesus. These activities are meant to enrich the time you spend with your children at home or in the classroom as you prepare for this blessed season. Most of the activities in this book involve baking and eating, representing culinary traditions and celebrations of Catholics around the world as they immerse themselves in the seasons and feast days of the Christian Calendar.

The environments that mothers and teachers find themselves in daily are diverse; the amount of time a mother may be able to spend on an activity with her children may be very different from the time a teacher has for any one activity in her classroom. With this consideration in mind, the activities and recipes that have been chosen for this book have suggestions for adaptations to the home, school, or CCD classroom.

In organizing this cookbook I have included information that might be useful as you plan a baking activity with your children, for instance, a section on cooking rules and safety. Level of difficulty and approximate time involved are included with each recipe. Liturgical colors appropriate to the season are in the back of the book. References for decorating artwork can be found in the Resource and Bibliography pages.

It is important to plan ahead when using this book. Looking ahead to Advent in late October or early November allows you to choose those activities that best suit your particular schedule to work into your Advent preparation. Do the same for the Christmas season. Choose activities about four weeks in advance to organize well-prepared celebrations. Two planning calendars are provided to help in scheduling.

❧ WORDS TO KNOW ❧

The following words and their explanations are included to assist you as you enter into the spirit of the Advent Season.

CELEBRATING AND FEASTING – We all look forward to celebrations, those joyful occasions when family and friends gather to honor, praise and rejoice in a person, an event, or a milestone with festivities. There are many times during the year that we celebrate special events such as birthdays, anniversaries, retirements, competitions, and national holidays. Christmastide presents ample opportunities for merrymaking, and thus, for teaching children the importance of the season through our acts of celebration.

In the Christian year starting with the Advent Season we have many occasions to celebrate. The examples of the saints, and Mary, Jesus' mother, inspire us and fill us with joy. **To celebrate means to observe a person or an event with customs of festivity and rejoicing.**

Children love to celebrate. They bring a naturally joyful spirit to brighten any occasion. In the home, school, or religious education classroom, one way to celebrate is with food. Over the centuries Catholics have prepared special foods to observe the feast days. In fact, one meaning of the word *feast* is a large, elaborately prepared meal!

Drawing on some of these food customs for feast days, and adding a few of our own, we observe the season of Advent. We celebrate its saints, honoring them for the virtues they achieved with God's grace and rejoicing in their victory over sin. We pray to them in heaven and ask for their help as we prepare to celebrate the birthday of Jesus. All of these celebrations and more help focus our minds and hearts on preparing for and rejoicing in the greatest event of the Christmas season: the birth of Jesus.

FASTING – is a type of discipline. **It refers to giving up food for a certain period of time or restricting the amount eaten.** It is a type of penance. Penance is any outward sign, gesture, or action that results from a heart converted to Jesus. Fasting aims at controlling the body so that we can concentrate on things of the spirit. Fasting is found both in the Church's present regulations for observing Lent and historically in the life of the Catholic faithful. During Advent the Church does not require the faithful to fast, but a person may do so if they choose.

ABSTINENCE – is a type of discipline. **It refers to refraining from eating certain foods.** In Lent Catholics are required to abstain from meat on Ash Wednesday and all Fridays. During Advent the Church does not command us to abstain from certain foods. (We are however required to abstain from meat on all Fridays of the year or choose another penance in commemoration of Our Lord's death on the Cross, *The Code of Canon Law*, canons 1251 and 1253).

As we prepare for the great feast of Christmas it is good to recall practices of Catholics in the past who avoided certain foods during Advent in order that they might save these delicious foods for the great feast of Christ's birth. An example of abstaining would be not to eat chocolate or some other treat during Advent, making the sacrifice and saving the chocolate or special treat for the wondrous celebration of Jesus' birth!

FEASTS – The Christian Calendar, also called the Liturgical Calendar, is sprinkled with feasts days. There are greater feasts and lesser feasts. **The word "feast" itself refers to a religious celebration in commemoration of some great event or person.** Christmas, the birth of Jesus, and Easter, the Resurrection of the Lord, are feasts of celebration in the Christian Calendar, Easter being the greatest feast of all. Together Christmas and Easter form the principal mysteries of the relationship between God and man. They are called Solemn Feasts and are indicated as such on the parish or diocesan Catholic Calendar we bring home from Church. The Church celebrates these two great events with special liturgies which include the Creed and the Gloria.

There are other days which are also Solemn Feasts. Each one commemorates a great saint or event central to the life of the Church. We should try to celebrate some of them in our homes and classrooms with parties consisting of special foods, fun activities, and music.

If you look on your parish calendar again you will see days designated as *feasts, memorials, and optional memorials*. These feasts are of a lesser rank than the Solemn Feasts but are still of universal importance to the faithful. At the Mass for a feast the Gloria is sung or said; it is not at the Mass for a memorial. An optional memorial is a feast that may be observed at the discretion of the priest. It is the feast day of a saint that the Church encourages but does not strictly require the faithful to celebrate. To summarize, the greater the degree of solemnity of a feast, the more essential is its celebration to the spiritual life of all members of the Universal Church.

LEGENDS - Some of the saints whose feast days we celebrate lived a very long time ago. Often there are few or no written records about them. The fact that the saint's feast day appears on the Universal Calendar of the Catholic Church testifies to his or her real existence and virtue; we can be assured that our celebrations are valid. It is true, however, that over the centuries many legends surround some of the saints. What is a legend? The famous hagiologist, Pere Delehaye, S.J., explains it in this way: "Legends presuppose an historical fact as basis or pretext...According as the preponderance is to be found on the side of fact or on that of fiction, the narrative may either be classed as history or legend." Some of the saints' stories, no doubt, are closer to legend than to history! This does not make the saint less a saint, but it does help us to understand not all "stories" that are told about some of the saints are based on fact(s).

SYMBOLS – A symbol is a thing that represents something else by association, resemblance, or agreement. It is usually a material object that is used to represent something invisible (spiritual). A wedding ring is an example of a symbol. It is a material object that represents the spiritual bond, the covenant bond, between the husband and wife. People who see a man or woman wearing a wedding ring know that the person is married.

In this book we have a few baking activities that focus on symbols of the Advent or Christmas seasons, e.g., the Advent Wreath. These symbols remind us of the deeper spiritual meaning associated with the season and, in our busy and distracting world, anchor us to the true meaning of Christmas.

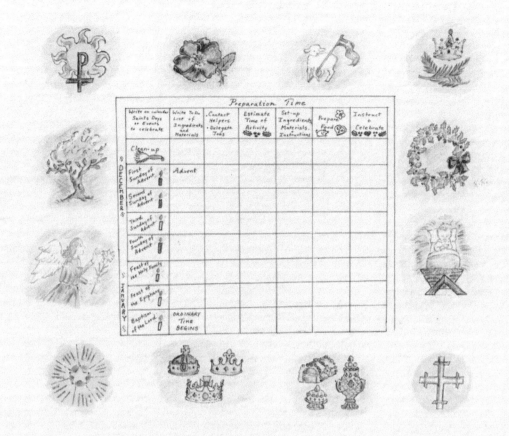

THE CHRISTIAN CALENDAR

We all live by calendars. We have the school calendar, the tax calendar, the sports calendar, the family calendar, and more. Calendars connect us with events that may require our action or demand our participation. The Catholic Church also has a calendar, the General Roman Calendar: it is called the Liturgical Calendar or, throughout this book, the Christian Calendar.

Maybe you have thought of the Church Calendar as simply marking past events in the life of Jesus, His mother, Mary, and the saints. The truth is the Christian Calendar focuses the faithful on honoring those who are living in the Church triumphant, *now*. The popes have taught, including Pope Paul VI in *Mysterii Paschalis* that these celebrations of the life of Our Lord, His Mother, and the saints during the liturgical year exert "a special sacramental power and influence which strengthens Christian life." The more actively engaged we are as Christians in participating in the liturgical celebrations of the Christian Calendar, the more fully we are transformed by the living Christ. The following is an explanation of the Christian Calendar.

The Christian Calendar is made up of twelve months, and its focus is the principal mysteries of the life of Jesus, His Mother, the angels, and the saints. The liturgical year begins on the

Sunday closest to the feast of St. Andrew the Apostle, November 30th. It is called the first Sunday of Advent and the Church season, the Advent Season.

The Advent Season comprises the four Sundays before December 25th. It is a season of joyful waiting and preparation for the birth of Our Lord. It is also the season in which we prepare our hearts to receive Christ and are reminded we are waiting expectantly for His Second Coming.

The Christmas Season begins at the Vigil Mass on December 24th and lasts until the Baptism of Our Lord. During the Christmas Season the Church draws our attention to the great mystery of the Incarnation and the transforming effect it is meant to have on our lives as we participate fully in the life of the Church.

The end of the Christmas Season signals the beginning of what the Church calls Ordinary Time. It is during this period, which extends until Ash Wednesday, that the great mystery of Jesus' birth among men is given time to mature deep inside of us through reading and meditation of the Scriptures, prayer, and reception of the sacraments.

Ash Wednesday is the beginning of the most important season in the life of the Christian: the season of Lent. It is during this season that the Church reminds the faithful of their immersion into the life of Christ at baptism. The Church also instructs those who are preparing to be baptized and to enter the Catholic Church at the Easter Vigil. The spirit of Lent is a penitential one in imitation and love of Our Lord who suffered and died on the Cross, so that we might be redeemed from sin and death. Forty days mark the period of time from Ash Wednesday to Holy Thursday. During this time we are called to unite ourselves to Christ through our prayers, mortifications, and almsgiving.

The Sixth Sunday of Lent, Palm Sunday, begins Holy Week. This is the most sacred week of the Christian year. It is during the later part of the week, the three days that precede Easter Sunday which are called the Triduum, that we commemorate Jesus' ordaining the Apostles as His first priests and leaving Himself in the Eucharist as the spiritual food for each believer on Holy Thursday. On Good Friday, we reverence His sufferings and death on the Cross for love of us and in atonement for our sins. Holy Saturday finds our churches empty, signifying the burial of Our Lord in the tomb and the separation of His soul from His body. The Triduum ends when the Easter Vigil begins.

The Easter Vigil marks the greatest and most jubilant season in the Church: the Easter Season. Christ has conquered death and is risen in a glorified state. From the Easter Vigil to Pentecost, there are fifty days of celebrating Christ's victory. The period immediately following Easter Sunday, Easter week, also called the Octave of Easter (eight days), is the most joyous period in the Christian calendar— in it we anticipate our own entry into glory.

Forty days after Easter Sunday we celebrate the Ascension of Our Lord into heaven. (In the United States many dioceses celebrate the Ascension on the seventh Sunday of Easter.) On Pentecost Sunday, as promised, Our Lord sent the Holy Spirit to His Apostles. The Blessed Mother and many holy women were present. This feast is the birthday of the Church and ends the Easter Season.

Ordinary Time resumes on the Monday after Pentecost, and it continues to the end of the Christian Calendar. The last Sunday of the Church year, the Thirty-fourth Sunday, is the great feast of Christ the King. The following Sunday will be the First Sunday of Advent and signifies the beginning of the new Christian year. To view *all* feasts in the United States for the current year, go to the Christian/Liturgical Calendar www.usccb.org/liturgy/current2013cal.pdf When the year changes, type in the new year. Liturgical calendars for other English-speaking countries may be found in the Resource section under Liturgical.

PLANNING CALENDAR

Four weeks before the start of each liturgical season is a good time to decide and plan which activities to try. You could observe Advent by making and baking an inedible Advent wreath, or preparing an edible Advent calendar. You might choose a saint such as St. Nicholas to honor for his generosity to the poor and his love of children while you bake and eat some of the foods associated with his feast day. Perhaps you will prepare for Jesus' birth by reenacting the search for shelter by Joseph and Mary in the Las Posadas custom as you eat some of the traditional foods associated with it. Whatever your plan, it is sure to be fun! The saints and events you observe are guaranteed to help you be ready for the great celebration on December 25th, the birth of Jesus.

You will find two planning calendars on the following pages to help you in your Advent and Christmas preparations. Copy them each year. Fill out the calendars with your plans, and then save them for future reference or to share with family and friends.

ADVENT & CHRISTMAS PLANNING CALENDAR

SUNDAY	MONDAY	TUESDAY	WEDNESDAY	THURSDAY	FRIDAY	SATURDAY

ADVENT & CHRISTMAS PLANNING CALENDAR

SUNDAY	MONDAY	TUESDAY	WEDNESDAY	THURSDAY	FRIDAY	SATURDAY

A LETTER TO PARENTS, TEACHERS, AND CATECHISTS

Dear Friends,

   The following page on Cooking Rules and Safety Precautions with Children is written to enhance the children's experience with baking. It is my hope that they will have opportunities to experience making and baking foods or a craft while learning good habits in the kitchen and having fun. My time in the kitchen with childen has taught me, that if you teach them safety rules and good habits, their youthful enthusiam will reward you with a creative display of attractive foods and crafts that will both amaze you and make you proud.

   Few of us like to clean-up, no. 7. This is a powerful habit and one that will make its practioner many friends! Since some of us rely on the use of rented or borrowed facilities to work with groups of children, it is a great habit to develop and, more often than not, ensures that we will be enthusiastically welcomed back.

   Happy Baking!
   Colleen

COOKING RULES
AND SAFETY PRECAUTIONS
WITH CHILDREN

1. **ALWAYS WASH YOUR HANDS** with soap and water. Then dry them with a clean towel or paper towel before handling food ingredients.

2. **WEAR AN OLD SHIRT** or an apron to protect your clothes.

3. **ADULT SUPERVISION OR PERMISSION IS REQUIRED** before you start the recipe. The recipes in this cookbook require the use of the stove, microwave, oven, knife, hammer, food processor, or blender.

4. **ADULTS:** Let the children do as much as they are able to do for their age levels and capabilities.

5. **READ THE RECIPE FIRST.** Follow the directions as stated. Levels of difficulty are included with each recipe.

6. **ASSEMBLE ALL INGREDIENTS** and equipment before you start baking.

7. **CLEAN AS YOU GO,** if possible. Otherwise, clean-up when you have finished the activity.

8. **READERS** from English-speaking countries using the metric system will find conversion tables for standard measurements to metric at **http://www.cakerecipes-r-us. com/baking-conversions.html**

⊰⊱ ADVENT SEASON ⊰⊱

In the Season of Advent, the Church stresses preparation for the birth of Christ. The word Advent is from the Latin, *adventus,* meaning "coming." Christians reflect on this period of waiting by preparing their hearts to celebrate Jesus' birth. The Season of Advent gives us many saints. The greatest saint among these is Mary, the mother of Jesus. The saints, particularly Mary, are special friends of Jesus. What better way to prepare for Christmas than to spend time with Mary and the saints?

So who would you like to spend some time with – will it be St. Nicholas, the patron saint of children, or the Blessed Mother under her title, the Immaculate Conception, or maybe Our Lady of Guadalupe, or St. Lucy, the teen, who gave her life for Christ? Perhaps you want to host a Posada Party like they do in Mexico, or prepare a skit explaining the Paradise Tree? Whatever you choose you are sure to have fun, waiting and preparing for the big day: the birthday of Jesus!

Wonderful as December 25th is, as the day draws to a close, don't make the mistake of thinking the fun and celebrating are over. There are eight days in the Octave of Christmas, and the Christmas Season ends on the feast of the Baptism of the Lord. Check out the fun foods you can bake, eat, and celebrate with – all Christmas long!

What can I give Him,
Poor as I am?
If I were a shepherd
I would bring a lamb,
If I were a wise man
I would do my part, -
Yet what I can I give Him,
Give my heart

by Christina Georgina Rossetti
(December 5, 1830 – December 29, 1894)

ADVENT WREATH

The Advent wreath as we know it has existed for a few centuries. It originated in eastern Germany among the Lutherans. Cartwheels wound in evergreens and decorated with lights were used by pre-Christians to appease their gods during the dark winter days in northern Europe and were probably the predecessors of the German wreath. The Advent wreath came to the United States in the late 1940s and early 1950s. It became popular in many parishes and homes and has since become a custom of Advent.

The symbolism of the wreath, circular in shape, stands for eternity – without beginning or end. Evergreens are an ancient symbol of victory and glory. The color green represents life and growth.

The four candles stand for the ages. Three are purple/violet, representing the first, second, and fourth weeks of Advent, and one candle is pink/rose for the third week. Purple or violet symbolizes penance, preparation, and sacrifice. The pink or rose candle, while still representing preparation and sacrifice, also stands for joy. We are joyful because we are halfway through our Advent preparation. The light of the candles represents Jesus, the light of the world. The act of lighting a candle each week signifies the growing power of Christ. Each adds more light until all four are ablaze, announcing the birth of Jesus Christ.

On Christmas Eve the colored candles are replaced by white ones, and a fifth candle—the Christ candle— may be added in the center, along with red and white decorative ribbons.

Here is a recipe for a nonedible, baked Advent wreath. You may either make one large wreath or a few smaller ones. Birthday candles are used for the mini wreaths. If you make the wreath the last week of November you should have it ready to use on the first Sunday or the first school week of Advent. A short Advent ceremony follows the recipe.

ADVENT BREAD DOUGH WREATH

(Nonedible: Recipe)

Level: Easy

PREP: 20 minutes   **BAKE: 1 hour**

INGREDIENTS   **EQUIPMENT**
4 cups of all-purpose flour   Large mixing bowl, Baking sheet
1 ½ cups of warm water   Floured board, Plastic, Foil, or Wax paper
1 cup of salt   Green & purple acrylic paint
                                         Clean paint brush
                                         4 candles (3 purple, 1 rose) or B-day candles for
                                         mini-wreaths

DIRECTIONS: **YIELD: 1 large or 6 mini-wreaths**

1. Combine flour and salt in bowl.

2. Make a well in center of flour/salt mixture.

3. Pour 1 cup water into flour mixture and stir. Hands will become sticky.

4. Add more water until flour is moist but not wet. Continue mixing. May use hands.

5. Knead dough 5 minutes on floured board until smooth.

6. Turn oven on to 325 degrees Fahrenheit.

7. Take the lump of kneaded dough and roll between hands making a rope of about 18 inches in length and 3 ½ inches in width. Attach ends to one another, making a fairly smooth seam by using a small amount of water to work dough together.

8. Place on an ungreased baking sheet. With one of your Advent candles, make four impressions 1- inch deep and about 4 inches apart.

9. Bake for 1 hour or until very hard. Let cool thoroughly before decorating.

DECORATING

1. Paint the wreath light green with acrylic paint.

2. Using the liturgical symbols in the back of the book, paint four different symbols for Advent beside each candle hole. You may want to use a dark green paint, or a purple paint for your symbols. Let dry.

3. Some people like to weave an artificial strand of store-bought evergreen around the bread dough wreath. The wreath may be set on a table or hung by purple and rose ribbons from a fixture – a chandelier, for instance.

4. Place your candles in the wreath after you have placed or hung it. A small amount of melted wax applied to the base of each hole may help the candles to remain firmly in place.

5. Change candles to white on Christmas Eve and include the Christ candle in the center of the wreath for those that are resting on a table! Ribbons may be changed to red and white.

6. Store in a cool, dry place after the Christmas season in a gallon-size plastic bag.

For the classroom with many children you may wish to make miniature Advent wreaths that each child can take home.

1. Give each child a lump of dough the size of a woman's fist. Roll between hands making a rope 10 inches in length.

2. Attach the ends, use a drop of water to work seams together.

3. Place on an ungreased cookie sheet. With a small birthday candle make four impressions, 1½ inches apart.

4. Bake for 40 – 50 minutes, until dry and hard.

5. You may use white birthday candles with purple and rose colored ribbons if you are unable to find purple birthday candles. Send the wreath home in a plastic bag with the Advent Ceremony, candles, and ribbons. Instruct the family to tie a purple ribbon in a bow around the base of three of the candles; tie a bow using a rose ribbon around the fourth candle.

CEREMONY

(Holy Water recommended—available at most Catholic Churches)

Prayers for Week One
Blessing of the Wreath
Leader: O God, through your Word all things are made holy. Pour down your blessings on this wreath. Give those of us who use this wreath hearts prepared to receive Jesus. May we receive every grace and blessing through Christ, Our Lord. Amen. (Leader sprinkles holy water on the wreath.)
First Candle is Lit.
Leader: O, Powerful God, increase our strength of will for doing good. May Christ find us eager to welcome Him at His coming and call us to His side in the Kingdom of Heaven where He lives with You and the Holy Spirit. Amen.

Prayer for Week Two
Second Candle is Lit.
Leader: God of power and mercy, open our hearts and remove those things that prevent us from receiving Jesus with joy. May we share in Jesus' wisdom and become one with Him when He comes in glory. We ask this through Jesus, our Lord, who is with You and the Holy Spirit, One God, now and forever. Amen.

Prayer for Week Three
Third Candle is Lit.
Leader: Lord God, may we your family experience the joy of salvation and celebrate the feast of Jesus' birth with love and thanksgiving. We make this prayer through Jesus Christ, Our Lord. Amen.

Prayer for Week Four
Fourth Candle is Lit.
Leader: Dear Lord, fill our hearts with your life. The angel Gabriel revealed to Mary the coming of Your Son as one of us. May we open our hearts wide by acts of charity in order to receive the Christ child joyfully on Christmas day.

O Come, O Come, Emmanuel

O Come, O come, Emmanuel,
And ransom captive Israel,
That mourns in lonely exile here
Until the Son of God appear.

Refrain: Rejoice! Rejoice! Emmanuel
Shall come to thee, O Israel!

O come, Thou Rod of Jesse free,
Thine own from Satan's tyranny;
From depths of hell
They people save
And give them vict'ry o'er the grave. *Refrain*

O come, Thou Dayspring, come and cheer
Our Spirits by Thine Advent here;
Disperse the gloomy clouds of night
And earth's dark shadows put to flight. *Refrain*

O come, Thou Key of David, come,
And open wide our heav'nly home,
Make safe the way that leads on high,
And close the path to misery. *Refrain*

The holly berry that burns so red
(Raise high the holly!)
Once was whiter than wheaten bread
(As love is better than folly.)

Villagers come there, half-afraid,
Gifts in their hands for Child and Maid.

And one has nothing of note, so he
Fetches a branch of the holly tree.

Alas, alas, the little Newborn
Has pricked His finger upon a thorn.

For sorrow and shame
The berries have blushed as red as flame
Says Mary the Mother,
"Take no blame."

Now red, rejoicing, the berries shine
On jubilant doors as a Christmas sign

That desolation to joy makes way.
(Hang high the holly!)
Holly is the symbol of Christ's Birthday.
(When love shall vanquish folly.)

from the *Legend of the Holly* by Phyllis McGinley
(March 21, 1905 – February 22, 1978)

✎ HOLLY ✎

This first holly wreath recipe, given to me by a dear friend, Myra Lindsey, is a favorite of mine. It is easy to make and very colorful to look at. The green-dyed cornflakes really give the appearance of holly leaves, and with a few red candies sprinkled around to look like the holly berries, you have both symbolism and edibility in a few easy steps.

Fr. Weiser tells us in his book, *Handbook of Christian Feasts and Customs*, that northern European Christians considered the holly as a symbol of the Burning Bush (see Exodus 3:2-3) and the flaming love for God that filled Mary's heart. Its prickly points and red berries, resembling drops of blood, remind us that the Divine Child was born to wear a crown of thorns. Today holly appears universally as a Christmas decoration.

HOLLY WREATH CENTERPIECE
(Edible)
Recipe One: Easy

PREP: 20 minutes

INGREDIENTS	**EQUIPMENT**
30 marshmallows	Double boiler or Coated 2-quart saucepan
½ cup of butter	Rubber spatula and Large spoon
1 teaspoon vanilla	Wax paper
2 teaspoons of green food coloring	Doily
3 ½ cups of cornflakes	
Red cinnamon candies or candied cherries	

DIRECTIONS:

YIELD: one 9-inch wreath or six 2 ½- inch wreaths

1. Combine marshmallows, butter, vanilla and food coloring in coated metal pan on medium heat. Heat until marshmallows and butter are melted, stirring frequently. Gradually stir in cornflakes.

2. Drop from spoon onto waxed paper. With lightly greased hands, shape into a 9- inch wreath. Decorate with red cinnamon candies or candied cherries. Place on doily. VARIATION: Drop cornflake mixture from teaspoon onto waxed paper. Shape with hands into tiny wreaths, about 1 ½ to 2- inches in diameter. Decorate with candies or cherries and place on small doilies.

HOLLY WREATH

Recipe Two: Easy

This recipe can be assembled and baked in a jiffy. It is ready to eat in about 25 minutes.

PREP: 10 minutes   **BAKE:** 12-14 minutes

INGREDIENTS
1 can refrigerated Cinnamon
Rolls with icing
Green food coloring
12 candied cherries

EQUIPMENT
Large cookie sheet
Knife
Serving plate or tray

DIRECTIONS: **YIELD: 8 servings**

1. Heat oven to 375 degrees Fahrenheit or temperature indicated on container.

2. Separate dough into 8 rolls; place with sides touching on an ungreased large cookie sheet in the form of a wreath. Bake at 375 for 12 to 14 minutes or until golden brown.

3. While wreath is baking, add food coloring to icing a drop at a time; blend well.

4. Remove warm wreath from cookie sheet; place on serving tray or plate. Cool.

5. Spread icing over wreath. Decorate each roll with 3 cherry halves. Enjoy!

❧ ADVENT CALENDAR ❧

The origins of the Advent Calendar can be traced to the nineteenth century. The first ones seem to have come from Germany and were made out of cardboard with little windows that were opened one by one, starting on December 1st and ending on December 25th. It is a charming way to progress through the Advent Season, particularly with younger children.

Today the Advent Calendar has many variations. Some have beautiful pictures from classical religious art with scriptural quotations behind each window. Others use religious folk art and scriptural quotations. Another group uses secular holiday pictures, decorative, or commercial pictures and counts down the days until gifts are received. A recent addition has been the edible Advent Calendar. Chocolate calendars, cookie calendars, all are now available. Most of these are severed from the true meaning of Christmas. In an attempt to reconcile creativity with meaning, included here is an edible Advent Calendar. We have left the most important feature of the Advent Calendar intact: the day-by-day scriptural journey to the manger. We hope you enjoy this new twist on a 19th century contribution!

ADVENT CALENDAR

(Edible: Sugar Cookie Recipe)

Level: Moderate with Mom's help

PREP: 20 minutes   **CHILL:** 1 hour   **BAKE:** 15 to 20 minutes   **DECORATE:** 30 minutes

INGREDIENTS*	EQUIPMENT
2 ½ cups all-purpose flour	Large bowl
¾ cup of sugar	Electric mixer
¾ cup of margarine or	Rubber spatula
butter, softened	Plastic wrap
1 teaspoon vanilla extract	Measuring spoons
1 ½ teaspoons baking powder	16" x 12" sheet graph paper
¼ teaspoon salt	Large cookie sheets
2 large eggs	Rolling pin
	Toothpicks, Paper for quotes, Glue gun
Ornamental Frosting	Wire racks
(recipe included), or	Decorator's bag with writing tips
Commercially prepared frosting	
Assorted food coloring, green sugar crystals	
And/or decorating gels	

DIRECTIONS: **YIELD:** Makes one calendar

1. In a large bowl, measure flour, sugar, margarine or butter, vanilla extract, baking powder, salt, and 1 egg. With mixer at low speed, beat ingredients until well blended, occasionally scraping bowl with rubber spatula. Shape dough into a ball; wrap with

plastic wrap and refrigerate 1 hour or until dough is easy to handle. (Or, place dough in freezer for 30 minutes.)

2. Meanwhile, on 16 x 12-inch sheet of graph paper, follow pattern enlarging according to scale, draw outline of the Christmas tree and dotted lines for Advent calendar days. Cut along the outline to make a tree pattern. (Pattern found after Scriptural Citations.)

3. Preheat oven to 350 degrees Fahrenheit. Grease large cookie sheet and sprinkle generously with flour. On cookie sheet, with floured rolling pin, roll cookie dough to ⅛ inch thickness to cover cookie sheet.

4. Place paper pattern on cookie dough; with knife cut out cookie tree and one small star-shaped cookie. Remove trimmings. Following dotted line on pattern, cut tree into 25 pieces, but do not remove the pieces. In cup, with fork, beat remaining egg slightly, brush lightly over cookies tree and star cookie. Bake 15 to 20 minutes until golden brown.

5. Remove cookie sheet to wire rack to cool five minutes; then with knife, cut through the calendar pieces. Make sure the cookie pieces are not attached to each other, but leave them in their original position on cookie sheet until they are cooled completely.

6. On another cookie sheet, reroll trimmings; cut out holiday shapes; bake to serve for snack or dessert. (You will have 25 cookies).

7. Decorate Advent Calendar cookies: prepare Ornamental Frosting. Leave a portion of frosting white. Divide rest of the frosting among several small bowls. Tint with food coloring as desired. Spoon frosting into small decorator's bags; place writing tip on each bag (wash and dry the tip after each use if you switch it from one bag of color to another).

8. Pipe white frosting on cookies along outer edges of the cookie tree; dip frosting in green sugar crystals to coat edges. With remaining frosting, decorate cookies and write numbers 1 through 24. Decorate the star cookie and with frosting, attach it to top of the cookie tree. You may either pipe on Scriptural citations or handwrite or type out the quotations on pieces of paper and attach each quote to a toothpick with a hot glue gun. They will look like flags. Place each completed tooth pick in a cookie. Have the children take turns each day reading the quote and eating the cookie. (Refrigerate between reading and eating!)

9. Let the decorated cookies dry at room temperature until frosting is completely set. Makes about 50 cookies, including cookies from the trimmings.

ORNAMENTAL FROSTING

In a small bowl, with mixer on low speed, beat one 16-ounce package of confectioners' sugar, ⅓ cup warm water, and 3 tablespoons meringue powder* until mixture is stiff and knife drawn through mixture leaves a clean-cut path. Thin icing if necessary with warm water, until it is of good piping consistency.

* Meringue powder is available in specialty stores or wherever cake-decorating equipment is sold. Go online to **http://www.wilton.com** for a store near you.

SCRIPTURAL CITATIONS

DAY 1   ISAIAH 9:2

DAY 2   PSALM 66:1

DAY 3   LUKE 1:38

DAY 4   LUKE 2:1

DAY 5   LUKE 2:9

DAY 6   MATTHEW 2:11

DAY 7   LUKE 1:35

DAY 8   MATTHEW 2:9

DAY 9   LUKE 2:20

DAY 10 LUKE 1:39

DAY 11 LUKE 2:4

DAY 12 PSALM 100:1

DAY 13 MATTHEW 2:10

DAY 14 ISAIAH 9:6

DAY 15 LUKE 2:13

DAY 16 MATTHEW 2:1

DAY 17 MATTHEW 2:3

DAY 18 LUKE 2:25

DAY 19 LUKE 2:18

DAY 20 LUKE 2:3

DAY 21 LUKE 1:46

DAY 22 LUKE 2:15

DAY 23 LUKE 1:26

DAY 24 LUKE 2:6-7

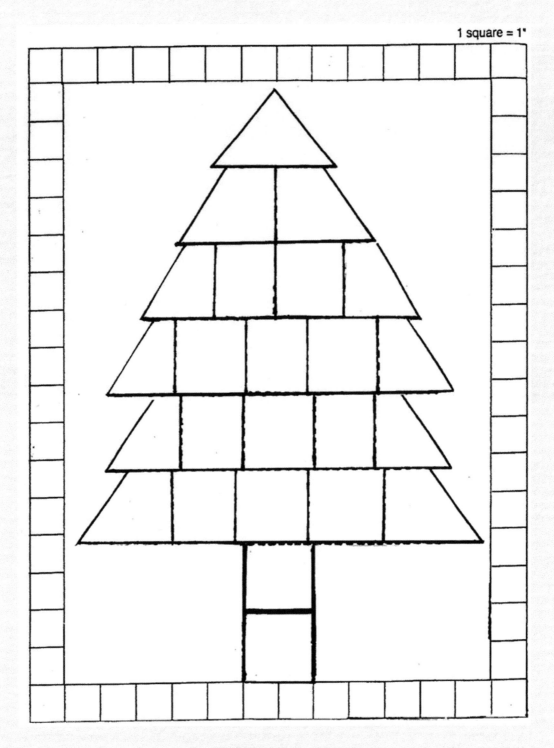

1 square = 1"

Advent Cookie Calendar Pattern

ST. NICHOLAS OF MYRA

Optional Memorial, December 6

Patron Saint of Children, Russia, and More

I cannot think of a better way to start off Advent than to honor St. Nicholas at a St. Nicholas party! St. Nicholas parties originated in Europe; they were popular in Germany, France, Belgium, Holland, Switzerland, England, and Ireland from the Middle Ages through the Renaissance. Children looked forward to St. Nicholas Eve, when they would put out their shoes or hang stockings in expectation of a visit, and a small gift from the saint. There are many legends about St. Nicholas and his goodness to the poor and needy, but I would first like to share a bit of what is truly known about him.

St. Nicholas of Myra was a fourth-century bishop from what is now southwestern Turkey. He is the patron saint of children. Little written evidence is available about St. Nicholas from the centuries closest to his death. However we have much evidence—in the form of church dedications, hymns, and mosaics fashioned in his honor—from very early on which tells us he was known and dearly loved by the people in his homeland and the surrounding Mediterranean region, all the way to Italy. Many miracles are attributed to his intercession; often children are the beneficiaries.

The height of St. Nicholas' popularity occurred in Catholic Europe after the transfer of his relics from Myra to Bari, Italy, in 1087. His feast day was observed by Catholics from Ireland to Italy between the eleventh and early sixteenth centuries. His life was obscured in Roman Catholic culture after much of Europe came under the influence of Martin Luther and John Calvin, who thought saints and festivals were something to be abolished. I am happy to say knowledge of St. Nicholas is making a comeback! You might like to read a story about his life or watch a movie to learn more about him during this Advent Season.

Fortunately, many of the food and party customs from the past honoring St. Nicholas have been lovingly handed down through the generations and are still known to us today. I have also included two contemporary recipes you might like to try. The following is a prayer asking St. Nicholas to help us on our journey to the manger in Bethlehem to meet the Christ Child.

Prayer to St. Nicholas

Heavenly Father, as Christmas draws near we commemorate the feast day of your beloved Bishop and Saint, Nicholas. We love and honor his memory because of his tender concern for children and the poor. We thank you for the merriment that his feast has brought down all the centuries. We ask you from the bottom of our hearts to help us to remember, on this, his feast day, that we should try to retain the innocence of childhood and a sincere faith in you all our lives. Show us, too, how to share the good things that we have with others, and to imitate St. Nicholas in generosity and goodwill. We ask him to pray for us from his place in heaven.

SPECULAAS COOKIES
(Spice Cookies)
Level: Moderate

Here is a yummy cookie that is associated with St. Nicholas Day in Holland, Germany, and Belgium. You may purchase pre-carved wooden boards into which you can press the dough and mold an authentic figure of St. Nicholas, or you can use St. Nicholas cookie cutters. Try this excellent recipe, reprinted from *A Continual Feast: A Cookbook to Celebrate the Joys of Family and Faith throughout the Christian Year* by Evelyn Birge Vitz, and add St. Nicholas cutouts of your own making!

PREP: 25 minutes   **CHILL:** 3 hours   **BAKE:** 10 to12 minutes   **DECORATE:** 10 to 15 minutes

INGREDIENTS
1 cup butter (2 sticks), at room temperature
2 cups dark brown sugar
2 eggs
Grated rind of one lemon
2 teaspoons cinnamon
1 teaspoon ground nutmeg or mace
½ teaspoon ground cloves
⅛ teaspoon ginger
⅛ teaspoon cardamom
⅛ teaspoon salt
4 cups all-purpose flour
1 teaspoon baking powder
Optional Icing (recipe included)

EQUIPMENT
Large bowl
Electric mixer
Large spoon or Rubber spatula
Sifter
Wax paper or Plastic wrap
Clean paint brushes for decoration
Cookie cutters,* Molds, Wooden board of St. Nicholas
Large cookies sheets
Wire racks

DIRECTIONS: YIELD: 3 dozen cookies

1. In a large bowl, cream the butter with the sugar until fluffy. Stir in the eggs one at a time, blending thoroughly after each addition. Stir in the lemon rind.

2. Sift the spices and salt with the flour and baking powder, and stir gradually into the butter mixture. Wrap in waxed paper or plastic wrap and chill for several hours or overnight. (If you are in a hurry, start the chilling process in the freezer: leave the dough in the freezer for about 20 minutes.)

3. On a floured surface, roll out the dough to about ⅛ inch. If you are going to make large figures – over 6 inches – you might roll out the dough a little thicker, to about ¼ inch; the figures will be less fragile. Cut out with cookies cutters, or with a sharp knife. This dough can also be used with a cookie mold, or can be molded by hand. (Follow the directions you received with your mold or board to form and bake.)

4. Place the cookies on lightly buttered baking sheets and bake at 350 degrees Fahrenheit for 10 to 12 minutes, or until set and lightly browned. Large or thick cookies will take somewhat longer and yield less than the 3 dozen listed. If you like your cookies soft, remove them from the oven when they are just set – the longer the baking time, the harder the gingerbread. Move from baking sheets to wire racks and let cool. Decorate. An icing recipe is given below.

OPTIONAL ICING

Place about ⅓ cup of powdered sugar in each of several small containers. Add a little bit of water and a drop or two of lemon juice or use egg white. Stir. Add a small amount of food coloring and stir until the consistency is fluid enough to paint with, but will not run all over the cookie. Apply with small paint brushes or a decorating tube. You can really let your creative imagination take over and decorate these as elaborately or as simply as you and your children like. *St. Nicholas cookie cutters may be purchased at **www.stnicholascenter.org**
*Adaptation: Use a refrigerated gingerbread or spice cookie dough as a substitute for making the cookies from scratch. You can cut them out and decorate them just like the ones from the recipe. Follow the directions for baking on the container or package.

BANKETLETTERS
(Initial Letter Cookies)
Level: Moderate

Among the many traditional foods that the Dutch make for the Feast of St. Nicholas, the initial letter cookie, or *banketletter*, is one the children look forward to year after year. A pastry-filled cookie shaped in the form of the child's first initial is found on the top of each child's shoe on the eve or morning of the feast. The customary Dutch filling is almond paste – you might try it, or perhaps a filling that is a family favorite. Below we include a recipe to make the pastry from scratch. If time is a consideration, a commercially prepared pastry and filling are suggested as quick alternatives.

PREP: 15 minutes   **CHILL:** 30 minutes   **BAKE:** 20 to 25 minutes

INGREDIENTS	EQUIPMENT
½ cup all-purpose flour	Small mixing bowl
4 tablespoons butter or margarine	Pastry cutter
1 tablespoon cold water	Measuring cup
½ cup almond paste or	Measuring spoons
favorite filling	Table fork & Cutting knife
1 egg beaten with	Plastic wrap
½ teaspoon of water*	Wax paper
¼ teaspoon vanilla	Cookie sheet
2 to 3 drops almond extract*	Spatula, Wire racks

DIRECTIONS: **YIELD:** a few cookies

1. Sift flour into a small mixing bowl. Cut butter or margarine into the flour with a pastry cutter. Blend the pieces into the flour with your fingertips until the mixture is like cornmeal.

2. Add the tablespoon of cold water mixed with the vanilla to the flour mixture, stirring it with a table fork. If you cannot form a ball with the dough, then add a little more water, ½ teaspoon at a time, but do not let the dough get sticky and soft.

3. Gather the dough into a ball, wrap in plastic wrap, and put in the refrigerator for 30 minutes to chill.

4. Place dough between two sheets of lightly floured wax paper, and roll out to $1/8$ inch thickness, keeping as near a rectangular shape as possible, with one side 5 inches long. Remove top sheet of paper carefully, and cut dough into strips, 5 inches long and 2 ½ inches wide.

5. Put almond paste in a bowl and add the almond extract, mixing it in with the fork. Taste a little bit to see if the flavor is strong enough. If not, add another drop or two of flavoring. Lightly roll paste with the palms of your hands on a clean sheet of wax paper, forming thin rolls $3/8$ inches in diameter and 4 ½ inches long.

6. Lift up one length of dough, place almond paste roll in the center, and bring dough around it. Close the long edge and each end with water, making sure they are well sealed. Repeat with rest of dough. Reroll any scraps into another strip.

7. Carefully form the rolls into letters of your choice, seam on the bottom. As you finish, place each one on a buttered baking sheet. When all the letters have been made and transferred to the baking sheet, brush them with the beaten egg.

8. Bake at 400 degrees Fahrenheit for 20 minutes. Check then to see if dough is light brown, and if not, check again in 5 minutes. When done, use spatula to transfer cookies to a wire rack to cool.

*Follow directions for commercially prepared pastry. Then insert filling. Shape into initial letter of child's first name. Brush with beaten egg. Bake according to the directions on the package. When done, transfer cookies using spatula to wire rack. Handle carefully.

Chocolate Filling   **Makes 1 Cup**
¼ cup whipping cream
½ cup semisweet chocolate chips
¾ cup powdered sugar, divided
½ teaspoon vanilla
Heat the cream and chocolate chips in saucepan over medium heat until melted and smooth, stirring constantly. Remove from heat; stir in ½ cup powdered sugar and vanilla. Stir in additional powdered sugar until filling is stiff enough to spread.

PEPERNOTEN
(Spicy Cookie Balls)
Level: Moderate

Here is another traditional treat children in the Netherlands look forward to receiving from St. Nicholas on his feast! The cookies are great for dipping in milk or dunking in hot chocolate.

PREP: 20 minutes   **BAKE:** 15 to 20 minutes

INGREDIENTS
3 tablespoons and 1 ½ teaspoons softened butter
½ cup of sugar
½ cup of dark brown sugar
1 tablespoon milk
1 cup of all-purpose flour
1 ¼ teaspoons of baking powder
¼ teaspoon of salt
1 teaspoon ground nutmeg
1 teaspoon cloves
1 teaspoon cinnamon
½ teaspoon ground aniseed
½ teaspoon ground ginger
Baking spray or shortening

EQUIPMENT
2 medium-size mixing bowl
Wire whisk, Large spoon
Measuring cups
Measuring spoons
Cookie sheets (2)
Airtight container
Electric mixer

DIRECTIONS: **YIELD:** 50 small cookies

1. In medium bowl, cream together butter and sugar. Add milk, mix well.

2. In other bowl, add flour, baking powder, salt, and all spices. Whisk together until are all incorporated.

3. Add flour mixture to sugar mixture and mix well. Add a small amount of milk if the mixture is too dry. Form mixture into a ball of dough.

4. Heat oven to 325 degrees Fahrenheit and spray or grease cookie sheets.

5. Break off small pieces of dough about ½ inch in diameter and roll in balls.

6. Place on cookie sheets and bake for 15 – 20 minutes, until light brown. Remove from oven and cool. Enjoy with a glass of milk or a hot cup of tea or cocoa. Store extra cookies in an airtight container.

GRATTIMANNEN COOKIES
(Little Bread Boys and Girls)
Level: Easy

In Italy, Switzerland, and other European countries on the Feast of St. Nicholas, it is traditional to bake delightful, edible, bread men with raisin eyes and decorative vests and caps of frosted dough or granulated sugar. Try this quick and easy recipe. You will be out of the kitchen and celebrating in a jiffy.

PREP: 30 minutes   **BAKE: 15 minutes**

INGREDIENTS   **EQUIPMENT**

2 ½ cups Bisquick®   Mixing bowl

½ cup milk   Large spoon

1 egg   Floured board

4 tablespoons vegetable oil   Large cookie sheets

1 cup flour   Gingerbread girl & boy cookie cutters

⅓ cup of sugar

1 teaspoon cinnamon

Seedless raisins, currants, or dried cranberries

1 egg yolk

DIRECTIONS: **YIELD: 15 boys and girls**

1. Mix ingredients (except raisins and egg yolk) until soft dough forms.

2. Roll the dough out thin on a lightly floured surface. Cut with a gingerbread boy or girl cookie cutter.

3. Transfer the cookies to a greased cookie sheet. Make hats, vest, boots, suspenders, nose, etc. from the separate pieces of the dough and assemble the bread figures directly on the cookie sheet. Attach these parts firmly with a bit of egg yolk and secure to the cutout. Press raisins into the dough to make eyes and onto the vests for buttons, or decorate in any way you might find appealing.

4. Bake approximately at 425 degrees Fahrenheit for 15 minutes or until lightly browned.

5. After the cookies are done, decorate with Ornamental Frosting (see Advent Calendar Recipe)   and add colored sprinkles, sugars, and candies as desired or sprinkle with granulated sugar. To view a picture of these little bread men go to cucinariodinonnaivana.blogspot.com/2011/2012. This blog is in Italian, but just hit the translate button and search for "little bread men." You will make a new Italian baking friend!

ST. NICK TREAT
Level: Easy

This recipe can be prepared in the classroom and then baked in a few short minutes. Be creative and try different kinds of refrigerated cookie dough and candy bars. It is sure to be a great hit!

PREP: 5 to 10 minutes　　　　**BAKE:** 10 to 12 minutes

INGREDIENTS　　　　　　　**EQUIPMENT**
1 ready-made refrigerated　　Large cookie sheets
cookie dough　　　　　　　　Knife
(slice-and-bake or dough in tubs)　Fork or cookie edger
2 chocolate-covered,　　　　　Wire racks
caramel-nougat
candy bars

DIRECTIONS:　　　　　　　**YIELD:** 20 treats

1. Preheat oven to 350 degrees Fahrenheit.

2. Slice refrigerated cookie dough into ¼-inch thick slices or use dough from tub and approximate the same size.

3. Cut each candy bar into 10 equal slices.

4. Place half the cookie slices 2 inches apart on 2 ungreased cookie sheets.

5. Put a slice of candy on each. Top with remaining cookie slices.

6. Press edges together with tines of fork or cookie edger, carefully sealing all edges of the cookies.

7. Bake 10 to 12 minutes or until lightly browned.

8. Cool slightly on cookie sheets until firm. Remove to wire rack to cool completely. Makes about 20 treats.

ST. NICHOLAS SQUARES

Level: Moderate

This recipe is sure to be a favorite, and it is addictive, too! **Caution: this recipe uses nuts. They may be omitted, and the squares will still be very tasty.**

PREP: 20 minutes   **BAKE:** 25 to 30 minutes

INGREDIENTS

1 stick unsalted butter or
margarine
1 ½ cups finely crushed
cinnamon crisp
graham cracker
crumbs (21 squares)
1 can (14 ounces) sweetened
condensed milk
1 cup (6 ounces) semisweet chocolate chips
1 ½ cups sweetened flaked coconut
¾ cup each unsalted Brazil nuts and
cashew nuts, chopped
½ cup semisweet chocolate Hershey's Holiday Bits®

EQUIPMENT

Aluminum foil
Baking pan, 13 x 9 inches
Rolling pin
Rolling surface
Wire racks
Cutting board

DIRECTIONS: **YIELD:** 48 squares

1. Preheat oven to 350 degrees Fahrenheit. Line a 13 x 9 inch baking pan with foil, letting foil extend 2 inches above pan at both ends.

2. Put butter in lined pan. Place in oven 3 to 5 minutes until melted. Tilt to coat bottom of pan.

3. Crush cinnamon crisp graham crackers with a rolling pin or in a food processor.

4. Sprinkle crushed grahams evenly over melted butter. Spread condensed milk over crushed graham crackers. Top with chips, coconut, nuts and baking bits. Press down gently.

5. Bake 25 to 30 minutes until edges are lightly browned. Cool in pan on wire rack.

6. Lift foil by ends onto cutting board. Cut slab into squares, remove from foil, and enjoy!

LESSONS FOR THE FEAST OF ST. NICHOLAS

The following is a format that may be useful for elementary school teachers, homeschoolers, or catechists when celebrating the Feast of St. Nicholas. It may be used for one class period or developed to include two class periods.

1. Instruct children to leave their shoes outside the classroom door. A classroom helper, out of view, should put some agreed upon treat(s) in one or both shoes while you teach the lesson. A holy card of St. Nicholas is nice to include with the treats.

2. Briefly introduce the life of St. Nicholas to the children.* You may want to follow it with a St. Nicholas video story, or a short skit. Some suggestions are offered in the Resource section at the back of the book.

3. Sum up the virtues that St. Nicholas excelled in – personal generosity, charity towards those in need, and care for the young and most vulnerable.

4. Send a letter home requesting that a pair of warm socks, mittens, or gloves be sent in for a St. Nicholas collection. These items may be brought in to class in the weeks leading up to Christmas. They will be given to St. Vincent de Paul, the Missionaries of Charity, or some organization that meets the needs of the poor.

5. Send the children out of the classroom a few at a time to get their shoes. When everyone has returned to their seats, they can celebrate St. Nicholas for his holy life and virtues by eating the treats.

6. End with a prayer to St. Nicholas. Remind the students he is the patron saint of children and encourage them to ask him to help us prepare our hearts to welcome the Christ child on Christmas day.

LESSONS FOR TWO CLASS PERIODS

1. Follow the format above using numbers 2, 3, & 4 for **first class period**.

2. **Second class period**: instruct the children to leave their shoes outside the classroom door. See number 1 above.

3. Collect the socks and mittens the children have brought in for the St. Nicholas collection. Briefly review the life of St. Nicholas. (Older children could discuss various ways to help the needy in your community.)

4. Make a treat to celebrate St. Nicholas' life and virtues. Discuss how he models Jesus for us by his love of the poor and his generosity with his own wealth. (Try the Easy Bake St. Nick Treat, or purchase something ready-made to eat.)

5. While the treat is baking or you are setting up to eat, send the children out for their shoes. You will want adult helpers to assist as the children find their shoes.

6. When everyone has their candy and treats, enjoy!

7. End with a prayer to St. Nicholas. See number 6 in lesson one.

Woman! Above all women gloried,

Our tainted nature's solitary boast.

from *The Virgin* by William Wordsworth

(April 7, 1770 – April 23, 1850)

FEAST OF THE IMMACULATE CONCEPTION

Solemnity, December 8

The Feast of the Immaculate Conception is one of the central mysteries and graces of the life of the Blessed Mother. On December 8, 1854, Pope Pius IX solemnly declared the dogma that Mary was preserved from Original Sin.

Just a few years earlier, in 1846, the Bishops of the United States at the First Council of Baltimore declared Mary patroness of the country. The Basilica of the National Shrine of the Immaculate Conception in Washington, D.C., the largest Roman Catholic church in the United States and North America, is popularly known as "America's Church." December 8 is a Solemn

Feast for all Roman Catholics and a holy day of obligation. It should be an occasion of great joy for all Christians because God became man by forming his body from the sinless flesh of the Blessed Virgin Mary.

This great feast occurs just a week or so after the beginning of Advent. Sometimes its celebration seems to get lost in the happy hustle and bustle of holiday preparations, at least in our home. In an attempt to initiate or rekindle the honoring of Mary in this great feast, a cookie, a cake, and a lollipop recipe are presented here. How wonderful it would be if many new recipes and traditions were established in honor of Mary's Immaculate Conception! It is hoped the readers of this book will create and share many ways in which we can celebrate this great feast of Mary – her Immaculate Conception.

HEART-SHAPED SUGAR COOKIES
Level: Moderate

The following buttery and versatile sugar cookie recipe is adapted from Tasha Tudor's Christmas book, *Take Joy!*

PREP: 20 minutes   **CHILL:** 1 hour or more   **BAKE:** 10 to 12 minutes

INGREDIENTS*
4 sticks of real, unsalted butter
2 eggs
5 cups all-purpose flour
2 cups sugar
A pinch of salt
1 tablespoon pure vanilla
1 teaspoon baking
soda dissolved in
3 tablespoons of milk
Frosting or icing

EQUIPMENT
1 large mixing bowl
Measuring spoons
Measuring cups
1 small bowl
Rolling pin
Heart-shaped cookie cutters
Clean rolling surface
Wire racks

Decorations: colored sprinkles, colored sugars, candies, candy flowers, candy ribbons, etc.
*May use ready-made dough instead.

DIRECTIONS: **YIELD:** 5 to 6 dozen cookies

1. Soften butter to room temperature. (Microwave for 5 seconds. Check to see if butter is softened. Repeat until *just* softened.)

2. Dissolve 1 teaspoon baking soda in 3 tablespoons milk.

3. Mix butter, eggs, flour, sugar, salt, vanilla, dissolved soda and milk in a large bowl with hands until the dough is smooth. The dough does not seem to be adversely effected by handling. Form dough into a ball, dust with flour and chill thoroughly before using.

4. Preheat the oven to 350 degrees Fahrenheit.

5. Break chilled dough into conveniently sized pieces. Take only the amount you want to bake for today. Add a bit more flour for ease in rolling out.

6. Dust the surface with flour. Place dough the size of an adult fist on surface. Roll out as thin as possible. Cut out with heart-shaped cookie cutters. Dust with colored sugar if desired (blue would be pretty, as it is often associated with Mary). You may want to make one or two very large cookies, also. Heart-shaped cookie cutters come in all sizes!

7. Bake on ungreased cookie sheet until light brown about 12 minutes.

8. Cool on a rack.

9. Decorate with frosting, pipe icing around the edges, drizzle chocolate, add sprinkles, or any tasty decorations that you like. Candied roses would be a nice touch.

HEART-SHAPED CAKE
Level: Easy

When you are in a hurry, nothing is easier than pulling a cake mix off the shelf and whipping up a quick treat. Cake pans come in all sizes and shapes, but our favorite to use when celebrating Mary's feast days is the heart-shaped pan. Most cake mixes will make two medium or one large cake. You can stack the smaller cakes one on top of the other and have a two-layered cake, or one large one-layer. Either way, you will have something tasty and easy to prepare to celebrate Mary's special day. Did you know in 2004 we celebrated the 150th anniversary of the dogma of the Immaculate Conception? In 2014, we will celebrate the 160th!

PREP: 10 minutes

BAKE: follow directions on mix

INGREDIENTS
1 cake mix
Water
Eggs
Vegetable oil or shortening
Floured spray
Prepared frosting or
whipped cream

EQUIPMENT
1 large mixing bowl
Measuring cups
Electric mixer
Large spoon or Spatula
Heart-shaped cake pan, Bundt pan,
or cupcake tins
Decorative plate or Doily

DIRECTIONS:

YIELD: 12 to 24 servings

1. Preheat oven as indicated on box.

2. Mix cake according to directions.

3. Spray or grease pan according to directions. Fill pan (or cupcake tins).

4. Place in preheated oven and bake as directed.

5. Remove from oven and cool. Be sure cake is fairly cool before removing it from the pan.

6. Place on decorative plate or a doily and frost.

7. You may want to color the frosting or add sprinkles to it. You can swirl food coloring into the frosting to give it various hues before you frost the cake. You might want to pipe "Happy Feast Day Mary" on the cake, or fill a decorative bag with frosting, add a decorative tip, and edge the cake all around! Whatever you decide, the end result is sure to be pretty and joyful.

LOLLIPOPS FOR MARY
Level: Easy

Heart-shaped lollipops are a very simple and beautiful treat for children to make in honor of Mary. If you are limited in the amount of time you have for a baking activity, but would like to do something with the children on this feast, you will find this recipe very easy to accomplish. I have made these lollipops with children as young as three and four years of age. The biggest challenge is to keep them from frequently dipping their fingers into the melted candy!

PREP: 5 minutes melting   **CHILL:** 15 minutes, or 5 minutes in freezer   **UNMOLD:** 2 minutes

INGREDIENTS
1 pound bag of white, red, pink or blue chocolate candy melts

EQUIPMENT
Heart-shaped lollipop molds (purchase at party, craft store, some Wal-Marts and online)
Lollipop sticks
Microwave or Double boiler
Large spoon for stirring
Smaller plastic spoons
Measuring cups

DIRECTIONS: **YIELD:** Varies according to size of molds

1. Melt about 1 cup of candy melts in microwavable bowl on high for 30 seconds. Remove from microwave and stir. If solid bits of candy remain, return to microwave and heat for 15 seconds. Remove from heat and stir until candy pieces are melted. If any pieces remain, return to microwave and heat for 10 seconds. Repeat until melted. **It is**

important not to burn the candy. Microwaves vary, so it is better to err on too little heat and time than too much.

2. Carefully pour out the melted candy, guiding it with a spoon into your molds. Molds should be filled completely. Be sure lollipop stick is placed in mold with melted candy completely covering it. Remaining candy can be reheated and reused.

3. Gently tap the mold to release air bubbles. You will see the bubbles rise to the surface and evaporate. Tap until no air bubbles remain.

4. Place molds in the refrigerator. The duration of time depends on the size and depth of the mold. Check every 5 minutes. You may place molds in the freezer, but unless carefully watched the candy has a tendency to crack when unmolded.

5. Remove candy from mold by gently tapping it. The lollipops are ready for eating. Enjoy!

6. For variety: you may decide to use two or more colors of melts and experiment with coloring different areas of the molds for decorative effect. With older children you can use clean, fine point paint brushes and paint details with the candy in the interior of the molds.

You may store extra lollipops in a plastic freezer bag in the freezer, if you don't eat them all!

LESSON FOR THE IMMACULATE CONCEPTION

Give a brief explanation to the children about this special day of Mary's. It might go something like this: Mary was conceived, "full of grace," in her mother's womb. Mary did not have Original Sin. It was a very special present that God gave to her because she would someday be the mother of Jesus, God's son. Only three human persons were created without Original Sin – Adam, Eve, and Mary. Adam and Eve sinned and lost God's grace for the human family. God promised to send a Savior to restore grace to mankind. Mary was conceived without Original Sin and she *never* sinned. She was full of God's grace all the time. Because Mary was *always* full of grace, she always said "yes" to God. Today we are celebrating Mary's Immaculate Conception and the fact she always was ready to do whatever God asked of her.

1. The Immaculate Conception is a great feast in the Church. It is a Solemn Feast and a holy day of obligation. Tell the children that we celebrate the feast first and foremost by going to Mass. We will also honor Mary today with a special party.

2. Make cookies using ready-made sugar cookie dough. Roll out the dough and cut out with heart-shaped cookie cutters. Explain to the children that these cookies represent Mary's heart, a heart full of love for God and for each one of us. When the cookies come out of the oven, after they have cooled for a few minutes, the children can decorate them with colored frostings, and all sorts of small candies. Have quite a few frostings, and candies to stress that this is a really special feast for a really special heart. If you do not have class time to bake cookies with the children, you could bring in heart-shaped cookies already baked but not decorated. Perhaps some of the mothers in your class would bake the cookies for you.

3. The children should wrap one or two of the special cookies to give to someone in honor of Mary's feast day—to Mom and Dad, or Grandpa and Grandma, a neighbor, etc. Then finish up the class by enjoying the cookies.

4. Give each child a prayer card of the Immaculate Conception and conclude with a prayer thanking Mary for always saying "yes" to God!

ST. JUAN DIEGO

Optional Memorial, December 9

St. Juan Diego was a member of the **Chichimeca** people of Mexico who became a Christian in 1524, when he was fifty years old. He was baptized by Fr. Peter da Gand, a Franciscan priest who was one of the first missionaries to Mexico. On December 9, 1531, on his way to Mass, Our Blessed Mother appeared to Juan Diego on Tepeyac Hill. She asked him to speak to Bishop Zumarraga in her name and ask for a shrine to be built at Tepeyac. She promised to pour out graces to those who prayed to her on that spot. The Bishop did not believe Juan Diego and asked for a sign. Juan Diego repeated the Bishop's request to the Blessed Mother. Mary told Juan Diego to climb the hill at Tepeyac and pick roses to bring to the Bishop. Roses were out of season in Mexico at that time of year. Nevertheless, Juan Diego picked many beautiful roses and put them in his *tilma*, a heavy woven shawl worn over the shoulders.

When he returned to the Bishop, Juan Diego opened his shawl, and the roses spilled out. More miraculous than the out-of-season roses was the image impressed on Juan Diego's *tilma* of the Blessed Virgin Mary as she had appeared to him at Tepeyac. (How the image was rendered on the *tilma* remains unknown. It was not painted. Scientists study it, but it remains a mystery.) The Bishop agreed to build the shrine, and the miraculous image of the Blessed Mother was hung there for the devotion of the faithful. Juan Diego, with the Bishop's permission, spent the rest of his life as caretaker of the shrine. He dedicated his life to prayer and the love of God and of neighbor. He died in 1548 and was canonized by Pope John Paul II in 2002. Today the image may be seen in the Basilica of Our Lady of Guadalupe, Mexico City, Mexico.

CHURROS
(Spanish Crullers)
Level: Moderate
Caveat: Hot oil

Churros are common throughout Mexico and are usually found at vendor stands on the streets. They are easy to make, but because of the hot oil for frying, only older children under adult supervision should be encouraged to take part in the cooking. Younger children can help prepare the ingredients!

PREP: 20 minutes   **FRYING:** 30 minutes

INGREDIENTS   **EQUIPMENT**

1 cup of water   Large frying pan

½ cup butter or margarine   Measuring cups

¼ teaspoon salt   Measuring spoons

1 cup all-purpose flour   3-quart saucepan

3 eggs   Large spoon

¼ cup sugar   Electric mixer

¼ teaspoon ground cinnamon   Decorator tube with large star tip

Vegetable oil for frying   1 roll paper towels

                                         Serving plate

DIRECTIONS: **YIELD:** 2 dozen *churros*

1. Pour oil to 1 ½ inches depth in large frying pan. Heat to 360 degrees Fahrenheit.

2. Heat water, butter, and salt to rolling boil in 3-quart saucepan; stir in flour.

3. Stir continually over low heat until mixture forms a ball, about 1 minute. Remove from heat.

4. With mixer, beat in eggs all at once; continue beating on medium speed until smooth.

5. Spoon mixture into decorator tube with large star tip in place. Squeeze 4-inch strips of dough into hot oil. Fry 3 or 4 strips at a time until golden brown, turning once, about 2 minutes on each side. Remove and drain on paper towels.

6. Mix together sugar and cinnamon; roll *churros* in sugar mixture and eat.

MOLLETES
(Cornmeal Cookies)
Level: Moderate
*Nuts

Corn is native to the Americas and a popular ingredient in the diet of indigenous Mexicans. It is a surprisingly versatile ingredient as you will see from this scrumptious cookie. I cannot think of a better way to celebrate the feast of St. Juan Diego and his great love of God and obedience to the request of Our Lady of Guadalupe than making and baking *molletes*. See if you don't find these cornmeal cookies, reprinted from Nancy Baggett's *The International Cookie Cookbook*, quite a treat!

PREP: 20 minutes

BAKE: 14 to 16 minutes

INGREDIENTS

¾ cup (1 ½ sticks) unsalted butter, slightly softened
⅔ cup granulated sugar
2 large egg yolks
1 ¼ teaspoons vanilla extract
½ cup white cornmeal
1 ¾ to 2 cups all-purpose flour or unbleached white flour, approximately

EQUIPMENT

Large mixing bowl
Electric mixer
Large spoon or Spatula
Measuring cups
Measuring spoons
Large wooden spoon
Cookie sheets
Wire racks
3 tablespoons pine nuts Airtight container

DIRECTIONS: **YIELD:** 35 two-inch cookies

1. Preheat oven to 350 degrees Fahrenheit. Grease several baking sheets and set aside.

2. Place butter in a large mixing bowl and beat with the mixer on medium speed until lightened.

3. Add sugar and beat until fluffy and well blended.

4. Beat in egg yolks and vanilla. Add cornmeal and beat until thoroughly incorporated.

5. Let mixture stand for 1 to 2 minutes.

6. Using a large wooden spoon, stir in 1¾ cups flour until the mixture is well-blended and smooth. Let stand for 5 minutes.

7. If dough seems too soft to shape with the hands, stir in a few tablespoons more flour; however, be careful not to add too much, as dough will continue to stiffen and dry out slightly as cornmeal absorbs moisture.

8. Pull out small portions of dough and roll between palms to form 1-inch balls.

9. Space on baking sheet about 1 ½ inches apart. Gently press each ball into a 1 ¾ disc with the heel of the hand. Imbed three pine nuts in a spoke-like pattern (with narrow ends toward center) on top of each cookie.

10. Place in the center of the oven and bake for 14 to 16 minutes, or until pale gold on top and lightly browned at edges.

11. Turn baking sheets from front to back about halfway through baking to ensure even browning. Remove baking sheets from the oven and let stand for 3 to 4 minutes. Then transfer cookies to wire racks and let cool completely.

12. Serve immediately. Leftovers can be stored in an airtight container for one week.

LESSON FOR ST. JUAN DIEGO

1. Today we are going to honor St. Juan Diego for his obedience to the Virgin of Guadalupe and for his perseverance in carrying out her request. You might watch the 30-minute video/DVD *Juan Diego: Messenger of Guadalupe* or read *St. Juan Diego and Our Lady of Guadalupe* by Josephine Nobisso. More resources are listed in the back of this book.

2. Antonio Valeriano, a native Mexican, wrote what was known about Juan Diego eight years after the saint's death. When the shrine was built on Tepeyac Hill as Our Lady requested, Juan Diego asked the Bishop if he might remain as its guardian. The Bishop agreed, and Juan Diego lived in a little hut near the chapel where the image of Our Lady of Guadalupe was placed for veneration. Juan Diego took care of the shrine and the pilgrims who came to pray to the Blessed Mother. When Juan Diego died, he was buried in the first chapel dedicated to the Virgin of Guadalupe. The image of Our Lady of Guadalupe can be seen today in the Basilica of Our Lady of Guadalupe, Mexico City, Mexico.

3. Explain to the children that the class is going to honor Juan Diego and ask for his help in preparing to receive Jesus at Christmas the way Mary, His Mother, did. St. Juan Diego is very close to the Blessed Virgin and is sure to help us.

4. Give out treats you have made or bought and then end with the prayer that appears on the following page.

Words from Our Lady of Guadalupe to St. Juan Diego

Listen, my son, to what I tell you now.

Do not be troubled or disturbed by anything; do not feel illness or any pain.

Am I not your Mother?

Am I not life and health?

Have I not placed you on my lap and made you my responsibility?

Do you need anything else?

St. Juan Diego, help me to grow closer to the Blessed Virgin.

OUR LADY OF GUADALUPE

Feast, December 12

Mary, the mother of Jesus, is patroness of the Americas under her title of Our Lady of Guadalupe. When Mary appeared to Juan Diego in 1531, she was clothed in a dress that had great significance to the indigenous people of the region. The sash on the dress signified that the woman wearing it was expecting a child. For this reason Our Lady of Guadalupe was chosen by Pope John Paul II as the Patroness of Life. The Blessed Mother also spoke in the native language of Juan Diego instead of Spanish during her appearances. The use of their native tongue endeared Mary to the Indians of Mexico. Huge numbers converted from their pagan religion to the Catholic faith following her appearances and the miraculous *tilma* image.

SOPAIPILLAS
(Fried Bread Puffs)
Level: Moderate – Adult Supervision
Caveat: Hot oil

These dough puffs, so popular in Mexico, are often found in a variety of geometric shapes. You can cut them out in the shape of stars to represent the ones on Our Lady of Guadalupe's mantle, or use your imagination to form other shapes.

PREP: 15 minutes   **CHILL:** 30 minutes   **FRY:** 20 minutes

INGREDIENTS	EQUIPMENT
2 tablespoons lard or shortening	Pastry cutter
2 cups all-purpose flour	Medium-sized bowl
2 teaspoons baking powder	Measuring spoons
1 teaspoon salt	Fork
⅔ cup lukewarm water	Candy/Frying thermometer
Vegetable oil for frying	Large frying pan
Cinnamon and sugar,	Rolling pin
confectionary sugar, or honey	Floured surface
Caramel Syrup	Roll of paper towels
3 cups water	Paper bag/Serving plate
1 ½ cups dark brown sugar,	Saucepan
¼ teaspoon anise seeds	

DIRECTIONS: YIELD: 18 puffs

1. Add flour, baking powder, and salt into medium-sized bowl.

2. Cut shortening into flour mixture completely with a pastry cutter.

3. Sprinkle in water, 1 tbsp. at a time, tossing with fork until all flour is moist and dough almost cleans sides of bowl. Form dough into a ball. Cover and refrigerate 30 minutes.

4. Place frying pan on burner and set heat on medium high. Fill oil in pan to a depth of 1 ½ inches. Heat oil to 400 degrees Fahrenheit. Check thermometer frequently.

5. While oil is heating, roll dough on lightly floured surface into rectangles, 12 x 10 inches. Cut into rectangles, 3 x 2 inches. Fry 3 or 4 rectangles at a time until puffed and golden, turning once, about 2 minutes on each side. **Or** roll dough into circles and cut stars out by hand with cookie cutters. Repeat. Fry.

6. Drain on paper towels. Sprinkle with cinnamon and sugar. You could also toss in a paper bag with confectioners' sugar, or drizzle with caramel syrup.

7. **Caramel Syrup:** Put all ingredients in saucepan. Turn heat to medium. Stir until sugar has melted. Bring to boil quickly. Let boil for 20 minutes. Remove from heat and cool. Drizzle over puffs or dip the puffs in the warm syrup. If you use honey, heat up the honey and drizzle or dip the puffs into it. It is very delicious!

Adapted from *Betty Crocker's Mexican Cookbook* by José Leopoldo Romero.

LEBKUCHEN

("Life Cakes")

Level: Moderate

*Nuts

It seems fitting to celebrate this feast with the traditional German bar known as *lebkuchen*. The folk etymology of *lebkuchen* is "life cakes." You can buy them in stores during the Advent and Christmas Seasons, or you can make them yourself.

PREP: 20 minutes   **CHILL:** 30 minutes, twice   **BAKE:** 30 minutes

INGREDIENTS	EQUIPMENT
½ cup unsalted butter, softened	Small, heavy saucepan
⅔ cup firmly packed light	Large mixing bowl
brown sugar	Large wooden spoon
1 egg, beaten	Electric mixer
⅓ cup of molasses	Cookie sheets
3 ½ cups self-rising flour	Rolling pin
1 teaspoon ground ginger	Lightly floured surface
½ teaspoon ground cloves	Knife
¼ teaspoon cayenne pepper	Wire racks
ICING	Wax paper or Aluminum foil
4 tablespoons granulated sugar	
⅓ cup water	
8 ounces semisweet chocolate, chopped	
¾ cup walnut halves	
⅓ cup candied cherries, chopped in small wedges	
1 cup whole blanched almonds	

DIRECTIONS: YIELD: 20 bars

1. Cream butter and sugar until pale and fluffy.

2. Beat in egg and molasses.

3. Sift the flour, ginger, cloves, and cayenne pepper into the bowl. Using a wooden spoon, gradually mix the ingredients together to make a stiff paste.

4. Turn onto a lightly floured work surface and knead lightly until smooth.

5. Wrap and chill for 30 minutes.

6. Grease two baking sheets.

7. Shape the dough into a roll, 8 inches long. Chill for 30 more minutes.

8. Cut dough into 20 slices and place 10 on each baking sheet.

9. Bake for 10 minutes at 350 degrees Fahrenheit. Leave on baking sheets for 5 minutes.

10. Transfer to cooling rack.

DECORATING* (Food allergy - Omit walnuts and almonds and replace with candied fruit)

1. Put sugar and water in small, heavy saucepan. Heat on medium until the sugar dissolves.

2. Bring to a boil and boil for one minute, until slightly syrupy.

3. Leave for 3 minutes to cool slightly, then stir in the chocolate until it has melted and made a smooth sauce.

4. Place rack of cookies over a large piece of wax paper or aluminum foil.

5. Spoon the chocolate mixture over the face of the cookies and around the sides.

6. Press a walnut half in the center of each cookie. Arrange cherries and almond around the walnut. Allow to set in a cool place.

LESSON FOR OUR LADY OF GUADALUPE

Explain to the children that Mary, Jesus' mother, has many feast days because with God's grace she has done many wonderful things for all people since her birth. Today the class is going to celebrate the feast of Our Lady of Guadalupe, when Mary appeared to St. Juan Diego, a native Indian of Mexico, in 1531.

1. Watch the 30-minute video/DVD (see Resource section of book) or read Tomie de Paolo's book on *Our Lady of Guadalupe*. There are other resources listed in the back of this book for older children.

2. Discuss the story with the students and point out to them the significance of the dress that the Blessed Mother was wearing. Mary was wearing a special dress that indicated she was expecting a baby. Life is a great gift from God. Explain to the children that the Blessed Mother is the patroness of the Americas—North, Central, and South—and she is the patroness of life. (**A patron is someone who supports, maintains, or protects another person, project, or enterprise.**)

3. Celebrate the gift of life that each child has been given from Jesus. Remind the children that this is the Season of Advent, when they are preparing to celebrate Jesus' birth. Jesus came so that we might have life and have it to the full (see John 10:10).

4. Buy some *lebkuchen* cookies or make some. Eat them in celebration of Mary's feast day as Our Lady of Guadalupe and remind the children *lebkuchen* means "life cakes"!

5. Here is a pro-life prayer you might pray together.

God, author of all life,
bless, we pray, this unborn child;
give constant protection
and grant a healthy birth
that is the sign of our rebirth one day
into the eternal rejoicing of heaven...
~ excerpt from the Prayer of Blessing

FEAST OF ST. LUCY

Memorial, December 13

There is not much written about St. Lucy. What is known comes from St. Aldhelm, an English bishop, who wrote about St. Lucy at the end of the seventh century. St. Lucy was born on the island of Sicily to wealthy Christian parents. Her father died when she was very young. She lived during the Diocletian persecution of the early Church, about 300 A.D.

Lucy was very beautiful, and as a young woman she vowed to dedicate herself to Christ and the poor. Her mother however, wishing an advantageous match for her daughter, arranged for Lucy to marry a pagan. The young girl was unhappy with this decision but had not told her mother of her desire to remain a virgin. It happened that one day, Lucy's mother became very ill. When she did not get better, Lucy suggested that they go to the grave of St. Agatha and pray for her recovery. It was after this visit that her mother's health was miraculously restored. Lucy then

revealed to her mother her desire to consecrate her life to Jesus and serve the poor. Her mother relented and agreed to Lucy's desire.

Lucy refused the proposal of marriage by the young pagan suitor, but her devotion to Jesus put her in great peril. Infuriated by her rejection, as well as the loss of her dowry, the young man publicly denounced her as a Christian. The imperial authorities demanded that Lucy honor the Roman gods and renounce her love for Jesus. She bravely refused and as a result was beheaded. During the reign of the Emperor Diocletian, Christians were persecuted terribly, and some accounts say Lucy's eyes were gouged out before the beheading. News spread far and wide of her heroic deed, and many miracles were received through her intercession. Missionaries told her story to the people of Scandinavia, and St. Lucy became a great favorite of theirs. St. Lucy's name means "light," and her feast day occurs in December, the darkest time of the year for people in the northern hemisphere. Many traditions associated with St. Lucy incorporate candles and lights. During a prolonged period of darkness, a celebration with lights is very cheery and lifts the spirits. St. Lucy is the patron saint of the blind and those with eye problems.

PEPPARKAKOR COOKIES

(Spice Cookies)

Level: Moderate

These traditional Scandinavian cookies appear on many St. Lucy day tables. You might want to display them on a beautifully painted plate. They won't last long. Try them and see! This recipe is adapted from *Kirsten's Cook Book*.

PREP: 20 minutes   **CHILL:** 30 minutes   **BAKE:** 8 to 10 minutes

INGREDIENTS*	EQUIPMENT
1 cup unsalted butter, softened	Sifter, Spatula
3 ¼ cups all-purpose flour	Medium mixing bowl
2 teaspoons baking soda	Measuring cups
2 teaspoons cinnamon	Electric mixer
1 teaspoons ginger	Measuring spoons
½ teaspoon ground cloves	Large mixing bowl
1 ½ cups sugar	Plastic wrap
1 egg	Rolling pin
2 tablespoons maple syrup	Baking sheets
1 tablespoon water	Cookie cutters
Extra flour for rolling out dough	Wire racks

DIRECTIONS: **YIELD:** 3 dozen cookies

1. Butter should be at room temperature.

2. Measure the flour, baking soda, cinnamon, ginger, and cloves into the sifter. Gradually sift ingredients into medium-sized bowl.

3. In the large mixing bowl place sugar and softened butter. With your spatula incorporate the sugar and butter.

4. Add the egg, maple syrup, and water to the butter and sugar mixture and beat with electric mixer on medium speed until fluffy.

5. Stir the dry ingredients into the wet mixture gradually. Mix well.

6. Cover the bowl with plastic wrap and chill the dough in the refrigerator for an hour or more, or in the freezer for 30 minutes.

7. Preheat oven to 350 degrees Fahrenheit.

8. Sprinkle flour onto a rolling surface. Cover the rolling pin with flour to keep the dough from sticking.

9. Divide the dough into 2 balls. Flatten the first ball and roll it from the center to the edges to ⅛- inch depth. For thicker cookies ¼ -inch depth.

10. Use cookie cutters to cut out shapes that are about the same size. Put the cookies 2 inches apart on the ungreased baking sheets.

11. Bake the cookies for 8 to 10 minutes until they are lightly browned on the bottom. (Slightly longer baking time if cookies are thicker than ⅛-inch.) Remove from oven and place on wire racks. Repeat process for second ball of dough or return to freezer for another day's baking.

*You may substitute refrigerated gingerbread cookie dough. Follow directions on the package. Roll out, cut with cookie cutters and bake as directed.

LUCIAKRONA

(Lucia Crown)

Level: Moderate

This is a bread machine recipe. Since machines vary, you may want to check with the booklet that came with yours to adjust the recipe. I am using a sweet bread recipe in the dough mode and completing the recipe by baking it in the oven. Since the bread machine allows you to omit the kneading process, this recipe requires much less effort—and allows more time for participating in St. Lucy's feast day fun.

PREP: 10 to 15 minutes   **MACHINE TIME:** 86 minutes   **BAKE:** 15 to 20 minutes

INGREDIENTS

	1- lb. capacity	2-lb. capacity
Water	½ cup	1 cup
Large egg	1 egg	2 eggs
Bread flour	2 cups	4 cups
Nonfat dry milk	2 tablespoons	¼ cup
Sugar	2 tablespoons	¼ cup
Salt	1 teaspoon	2 teaspoons
Unsalted butter	¼ cup	½ cup
Active dry yeast	1 ½ teaspoons	1 tablespoon

EQUIPMENT

Bread machine
Measuring cups
Measuring spoons
Rolling surface
Pastry brush
Baking sheets
Wire racks
Pastry brush

Egg Yolk Glaze
1 egg yolk
1 tablespoon water

Icing
1 cup confectionary sugar
1 tablespoon lemon juice
2 teaspoons grated lemon zest
1 tablespoon milk

Decorations
⅓ cup raisins or
dried craisins® or
lingonberry jam

DIRECTIONS: **YIELD:** one or two large bread crowns

1. Place ingredients into the bread pan. Place bread pan into the bread machine.

2. Select the DOUGH MODE and appropriate capacity. Press the START button. When the beeper sounds, press the STOP button and remove the bread pan from the bread machine. (If your bread machine's directions are different for the dough mode, follow them.) Remove dough from bread pan. Place on floured surface.

3. Form dough into one ball for 1-lb. capacity, (2 balls for 2-lb. capacity). Let rest for 10 minutes. Directions that follow are for the 2-lb. capacity, yielding two large bread crowns.

4. From the 2 balls, break into six equal chunks of dough. First roll one chunk of dough between your hands into a ball. Then roll the ball into an 18-inch rope. Set aside. Repeat with the other five chunks. You will have six ropes.

5. Take three of the ropes and pinch together at one end and begin braiding. Continue braiding until you reach the ends. Pinch the ends together. Take one end of the braid and attach to the other end of the braid by pinching together. You may use a bit of water, milk, or beaten egg yolk as an adhesive to hold the ends together. Your braid should form a crown. Place braided bread crown on lightly greased baking sheet.

6. For second bread crown, repeat the previous step with the remaining dough.

7. Cover both bread crowns with a dish towel and let rise in a warm place for 50 to 60 minutes, until double in size.

8. For egg yolk glaze, add one tablespoon of water to beaten egg yolk. Gently brush glaze on bread crowns before baking. Bake in preheated oven at 400 degrees Fahrenheit for 15 minutes to 20 minutes, until golden brown. Cool.

9. Icing. Combine ingredients in a small bowl and then drizzle over bread crown. Dot with raisins or craisins®, or drizzle with warm lingonberry jam. Serve for breakfast on the Feast of St. Lucy or any other time of the year!

ST. LUCIA BUNS
Level: Moderate

Who wouldn't like to wake to the aroma of St. Lucia buns wafting throughout the home? Traditionally the oldest daughter in the family brings a lovely breakfast of delicious buns and hot coffee to her parents on the Feast of St. Lucy. No daughters in the family? Your sons can do it, too!

PREP: 20 minutes

BAKE: 15 to 20 min.

INGREDIENTS*
⅓ cup milk
¼ cup of unsalted butter
¼ cup lukewarm water
1 package dry yeast
(2 ¼ tsp of yeast)
¼ cup sugar
1 egg
½ teaspoon salt
¼ teaspoon saffron
2 ¾ cups flour
1 tablespoon cooking oil
1 egg
1 tablespoon water
Raisins (24)

EQUIPMENT
Measuring cups
Measuring spoons
Small saucepan
Knife
Cutting board
Wooden spoon
Large mixing bowl
Baking sheet
Fork
Small bowl
Pastry brush
Wire racks

DIRECTIONS:

YIELD: 6 buns

1. Pour milk into a small saucepan over low heat. Cut in butter and stir until melted. Remove from heat and set aside.

2. Measure the lukewarm water (approximately 100-110 degrees Fahrenheit) into the large mixing bowl. Sprinkle the yeast over the water. Stir and let rest for 5 minutes.

3. Add the milk and buttery liquid to the yeast. Stir in the sugar, egg, salt, and saffron. Add 1 ½ cups of flour and stir until smooth.

4. Shape the dough into a ball with remaining flour, saving some flour for kneading the dough.

5. Place dough on floured cutting board surface. Dust hands with flour and knead dough until smooth - 5 to 10 minutes. If dough becomes sticky, add more flour, but not too much. (I often use my stand mixer with the dough hook to do the bulk of the kneading for me!)

6. Dough will form into a smooth ball. It should spring back when you poke it with your finger.

7. Place the dough in a large, lightly oiled bowl. Roll the dough until it is entirely coated. Cover and set in a warm place for about 45 minutes. Dough should double in size. Increase time until it is doubled.

8. Once dough has doubled in size, punch it down. Then divide it into 6 sections. Take 1 section and divide it in half. Roll each half into an 8-inch rope. Cross the 2 ropes in the middle. Then coil the ends in a tight circle. Shape the remainder of buns in the same way.

9. Place buns on greased cookie sheet, 2 inches apart. Cover and let rise for 30 to 45 minutes, until double in size.

10. Preheat the oven to 350 degrees Fahrenheit.

11. Mix the egg and water with a fork in a small bowl. Brush this mixture over the top of each bun. Decorate the buns with raisins. Raisins will stick to dough if egg mixture is used like glue to help them adhere.

12. Bake the buns for 15 to 20 minutes. When the buns are golden brown, remove from oven and place on wire rack to cool. Yum! Drizzle with icing or jelly if desired. This recipe is adapted from *Kirsten's Cook Book*.

*REFRIGERATED CINNAMON BUNS SUBSTITUTE: Use refrigerated cinnamon buns in place of dough. Place buns on cookie sheet, attaching buns one to another in a circle. Follow baking directions. When done, remove from oven, cool slightly, and then drizzle packaged icing over buns. Add decorative cherries if desired, place on plate, and serve. Quick, easy, and tasty!

ST. LUCY'S "EYEBALLS"
Level: Easy

What little baker wouldn't find this tasty treat fun to make and delightfully mischievous to offer to friends?

PREP: 2 minutes

MICROWAVE: 15 second intervals

INGREDIENTS
Wagon-wheel-shaped pretzels
Hershey's Candy Cane Kisses®
Mint Chocolate M & M's®
or your favorite color

EQUIPMENT
Dessert-size paper plates
Microwave

DIRECTIONS:

YIELD: Many eyeballs!

1. Place a number of wagon wheel-shaped pretzels on dessert-size paper plate. On top of each pretzel place a Hershey's Candy Cane Kiss®. Microwave in 15-second intervals until the kiss is soft but not runny.

2. Remove from microwave. Place one M & M® in the center of the soft kiss. Let cool and harden. Share with family and friends.

LESSON FOR THE FEAST OF ST. LUCY

1. Explain to the children that today we celebrate St. Lucy's feast because she was such a brave young girl. Retell the story of St. Lucy or read the legend from *Lucia Child of Light*, by Florence Ekstrand. St. Lucy is a special friend to children because she herself was young when she gave her life for love of Jesus. St. Lucy is a small light burning brightly during the Advent Season, leading us to the Great Light, Jesus.

2. Make a St. Lucy crown with ready-made cinnamon dough available in your grocer's freezer section. Assemble the children in pairs. Take the dough out of the cans. Place one bun at each child's spot. Show the children how to roll the bun into a rope about six inches long. You may need to have a small bit of flour on hand so the dough won't be too sticky. Tell the children to lightly sprinkle a little flour on the bun before they roll it so it won't stick. Then have each child intertwine his or her rope with the partner's, shaping it into a crown. Pinch the ends together. Follow the instructions for baking on the container, about 15 minutes. When the crowns come out of the oven, you may cool them for a few minutes and then frost with prepackaged icing. Eat and enjoy!

3. End the class by asking each child to pray to St. Lucy for the gift of light—the light to see Jesus and to prepare their hearts to celebrate His birthday joyfully at Christmas.

PREPARATIONS FOR THE BIRTH OF CHRIST

December 17-24

Beginning on December 17th, there is a shift in emphasis in the liturgical readings of the Church. This shift is particularly evident in the Church's use of the O Antiphons and reflects a heightened anticipation of the celebration of the birth of the long-awaited Messiah. We recall liturgically the period of waiting from the promise given to our first parents (see Genesis 3:15), the promise of a Savior, to the birth of Our Lord, the long-awaited Messiah (see Luke 2:1-7). The O Antiphons are taken from the Old Testament prophecies of the future Messiah, the one who would save His people from sin and death. On each of the seven days before Christmas, an Old Testament prophecy is included in the liturgy of the day.

In the week before Christmas, there is a parallel anticipation among children, families, and society as each awaits the Christmas celebrations. Even nature seems to deck herself out in a trimming of snow in the northern hemisphere or a garland of flowers in the southern hemisphere in anticipation of the nativity of the Lord.

It is only natural within the rhythm of preparation to fill it with activities that reflect the spirit of the week: anticipation, increased prayer, and a deepening sense of wonder. The following pages include some pre-Christmas traditions found throughout the Christian world: Las Posadas, Simbang Gabi, and the Paradise Play, along with a variety of baking and decorating projects to keep family and friends enjoying the time together as they prepare to celebrate the birth of Christ.

Vamos, Pastores, Vamos
Come, Shepherds, Come
(English Translation)

Come, shepherds, come to Bethlehem,

See where Jesus lies;

See him whose birth has saved us,

Glory of paradise

See him whose birth has saved us,

The joy of paradise

Beautiful baby Jesus,

I'd gladly die for him;

His shining eyes delight me,

Each perfect little limb

Joseph so gently strokes him;

Mary looks on in joy;

Caught up both in sweet rapture,

Worship their infant boy.

Composed by E. Ciria

LAS POSADAS

December 16-24

This wonderful Mexican tradition originally occurred over nine evenings. The word *posadas* means "inns" or "lodgings." The tradition of *Las Posadas* developed during the sixteenth century, the Colonial period in Mexico's history. Spanish missionaries brought customs from their country and adapted customs of the Indians for Christmas celebrations.

The Aztecs celebrated the arrival of Huitzilopochtli, their god of sun and war, between December 7th and 26th. Brother Pedro de Gante, a Franciscan and one of the first missionaries to the New World, documented this celebration in 1528. Festivities included songs, poetry, a battle of warriors, huge feasts, and torch-lit processions. Under Spanish rule, Catholic priests transferred some days of the ancient Aztec tradition to a new set of Catholic celebrations.

The Aztec Indians reenacted important historical events and real-life stories through plays. Missionaries incorporated this practice to present the events from the life of Jesus. These plays,

or *pastorelas,* occurred at the end of special Masses known as *aguinaldos,* "Christmas present Masses." These nine Masses, or novena, were begun on December 16 and ended on December 24. At the end of Mass, *piñatas* were broken, people sang songs *(villancios),* and they watched the *pastorelas. Nacimientos,* pictures of Jesus' birth, were on display for everyone to venerate. These were truly festive celebrations!

Las Posadas is a *pastorela.* It is a reenactment of Joseph's search for lodging for Mary and himself during their trip to Bethlehem as Mary awaited the birth of Jesus (Luke 2: 4–7.) Over the years, *Las Posadas* has been adapted in various ways. More often than not, it now takes place on one evening; however, in the past it took place over nine evenings. It usually begins in a neighborhood, with family and friends gathered together. Adults carry candles, and all sing the Litany of the Virgin Mary. Two children may be dressed as Mary and Joseph, or two representations of Mary and Joseph are carried by the children. A few persons, the hosts, remain inside the final home. The remainder of the group processes around from house to house, singing a song, asking for lodging. At eight homes they request lodging for Mary and Joseph and are refused. At the ninth home the host offers Mary and Joseph a place to stay. All enter the home, where baby Jesus is placed in the Nativity set, and a novena is recited. The guests then sing a song asking to break the piñata, and the fun begins! In some homes, a festive dinner is served after the breaking of the piñata. In most homes the custom is to give out *colación,* small baskets filled with treats – candy, toys, or fruit. There is much singing of Mexican Christmas carols, and a merry spirit reigns among family and friends.

BUÑUELOS
(Mexican Fried Cakes)
Level: Moderate (Caution—Hot Oil)

Buñuelos are traditional pastries which are served throughout the Christmas Season in Mexico. During the Spanish Colonial period, Religious Sisters experimenting with various ingredients concocted these delicious fritters. They are a big treat on the Feast of the Virgin of Solitude, Oaxaca's patron saint whom Mexicans honor on December 17th. Custom has it that the plate on which the *buñuelo* is served is smashed on the ground after the fritter is eaten! This recipe is adapted from *A Continual Feast* by Evelyn Birge Vitz.

PREP: 15 minutes   **RISE:** 20 minutes   **FRYING:** 30 minutes

INGREDIENTS	EQUIPMENT
4 cups all-purpose flour	Large mixing bowl
2 tablespoons sugar	Sifter
1 teaspoon baking powder	Large measuring cup
1 teaspoon salt	Large spoon
2 eggs	Electric mixer
¾ cup milk	Small mixing bowl
1 to 2 tablespoons crushed	Small saucepan or
anise seeds or	microwavable bowl
grated rind of one lemon or	Floured surface
½ orange (optional)	Large frying pan
¼ cup melted butter	Candy/frying thermometer
Vegetable oil for deep-fat frying	
Confectioners' sugar and cinnamon,	
granulated sugar and cinnamon, anise	
seeds, or honey	

DIRECTIONS

YIELD: 18 to 24 fritters

1. In a large bowl, sift the flour with the sugar, baking powder, and salt.

2. In a small bowl, beat eggs with the milk and stir them into the dry ingredients.

3. Add flavoring (anise, lemon, or ½ grated orange) if desired.

4. Melt butter in small microwavable container, or on stove in small saucepan.

5. Add melted butter to ingredients in large bowl.

6. Turn the dough onto a floured surface and knead for 5 to 10 minutes, or until very smooth. Add more milk or more flour, if necessary.

7. Divide the dough into 20 to 24 pieces. Shape into balls.

8. Cover the balls with a light cloth for 15 to 20 minutes.

9. On a lightly floured surface, roll each ball out into a very thin, large circle about the size of a tortilla.

10. Heat the oil to 370 degrees Fahrenheit. Test temperature of oil with thermometer. Fry the *buñuelos* three or four at a time in the hot oil, turning once or twice, until puffed and golden brown. Drain thoroughly on paper towels.

11. Serve hot. Mix the cinnamon and sugar in a paper bag. Place the *buñuelos* in the bag and gently toss until each is coated with the mixture, or serve with honey. Try both!

BIZCOCHITOS
(Sugar Cookies)

Level: Moderate

Bizcochitos are sugar cookies from New Mexico, traditionally cut out in the shape of fleurs-de-lis. Many recipes call for lard, but here we are using shortening instead. *Bizcochitos* are enjoyed at *Las Posadas* celebrations in Hispanic communities throughout the United States. Try these tasty cookies as you search with Mary and Joseph for lodging for the Christ Child.

PREP: 15 minutes   **BAKE: 10 – 12 minutes**

INGREDIENTS   **EQUIPMENT**

¾ cup of sugar   Measuring cups

1 teaspoon cinnamon   Measuring spoons

1 cup vegetable shortening   Mixing bowls

1 egg   Sifter & Wooden spoon

1 ½ teaspoon anise seeds   Pastry cutter or Fork

3 cups flour   Rolling pin

1 ¾ teaspoon baking powder   Cookie cutters

½ teaspoon salt   Spatula

1 teaspoon vanilla   Cookie sheets

2 to 3 teaspoons cold water   Wire racks

Electric mixer

DIRECTIONS: **YIELD:** 5 dozen cookies

1. Mix ¼ cup of sugar with 1 teaspoon of cinnamon in small bowl. Set aside.

2. In second bowl, with electric mixer, mix 1 cup of shortening with ½ cup of sugar until mixture is light and fluffy.

3. Add egg into mixture and mix well. Add anise seed and stir thoroughly. Set aside.

4. Place sifter in third bowl. Add flour, baking powder, and salt into sifter, then sift ingredients.

5. Add flour mixture to the shortening and sugar mixture. Use pastry cutter or fork to cut the shortening into the flour until the mixture is crumbly.

6. Add vanilla. Add just enough water to hold the dough together. Do not moisten too much.

7. Divide dough into 3 balls. Refrigerate 2 balls.

8. Flour the rolling surface and flour the rolling pin.

9. Roll out the first ball of dough from the center to the edge to about ¼- inch thickness.

10. Cut shapes out with cookie cutters. Sprinkle with the sugar and cinnamon mixture.

11. Bake cookies 10 to 12 minutes at 375 degrees Fahrenheit until lightly browned on the bottom.

12. Remove cookies from baking sheet. Place on wire cooling racks and sprinkle with more sugar.

13. Repeat process with second and third balls of dough.

MEXICAN HOT CHOCOLATE
Level: Easy

Round tablets of real Mexican chocolate are available in most supermarkets in the United States—Ibarra and Abuelita are both popular brands. The tablets are flavored with cinnamon, vanilla, and often ground almonds and are sweetened with sugar. I've included two hot chocolate recipes here. One uses the tablets; the other uses individual ingredients. Be sure to try both!

Mexican Hot Chocolate Recipe 1

Careful: Hot Milk

PREP: 5 to 7 minutes

INGREDIENTS	EQUIPMENT
4 cups milk	Small saucepan
1 Abuelita tablet	Measuring cups
Sugar to taste	Spoon for stirring
	Blender

DIRECTIONS: **YIELD:** 4 cups

1. Heat milk in saucepan. Stir until hot but not boiling.

2. Place one Abuelita tablet in the blender. Add hot milk and sugar to taste.

3. Blend until well-mixed. Serve hot.

Mexican Hot Chocolate Recipe 2

Careful: Hot Milk

PREP: 10 minutes

INGREDIENTS	EQUIPMENT
4 to 6 ounces plain chocolate, broken	Small saucepan
½ teaspoon ground cinnamon	Measuring spoons
4 cups milk	Measuring cups
Dash almond extract	Wire whisk
Few grains salt	Grater
Sugar to taste	
Chocolate for grating	
4 cinnamon sticks	

DIRECTIONS: **YIELD:** 4 cups

1. Heat chocolate with cinnamon and milk in saucepan on low.

2. When the chocolate has melted, add almond and vanilla extracts, along with the salt and sugar. Whisk together well and heat thoroughly.

3. Pour into cups, sprinkle with grated chocolate and serve with cinnamon sticks.

LESSON FOR LAS POSADAS

1. The entire class period could be devoted to the reenactment of *Las Posadas* with a traditional Mexican treat at the end – perhaps hot chocolate and *buñuelos* or *churros*.

2. Prepare the children (and their families if you invite them beforehand) with the following description of the *Las Posadas* custom.

3. *Las Posadas* is a reenactment of the search by Joseph for lodging for Mary shortly before Jesus was born. During the search, Joseph requests a place to stay at eight different locations, and eight times he is refused. On the ninth occasion, Joseph asks and is offered entry. He and Mary gratefully accept the lodging, and after they settle in, the Christ Child is born. The baby is placed in the manger. Jesus' birth is first celebrated with a prayer, followed by songs. Next, food and a piñata are brought out. The piñata is broken open, and all receive some treats.

4. The setting for *Las Posadas* may be a home, a school, or neighborhood. The nine locations that Joseph and Mary visit during the *Las Posadas* procession may be represented by nine locations in a house, nine classrooms or stations in a school, or nine different homes in a neighborhood.

5. Choose two children to be Joseph and Mary. You may choose more children and have the children take turns being Joseph and Mary, or simply have them act as companions who are in the party seeking lodging. Other children may take the parts of the eight innkeepers who refused Joseph. The ninth and final innkeeper is located at the last station where the procession ends with the baby Jesus being placed in a manger. Mary and Joseph finally rest. A prayer is said to the Christ Child. If you have time and space, a piñata is a nice treat. A star- shaped piñata is appropriate and very traditional.

6. End with a treat and a small gift – a prayer card of the Holy Family or the Christ Child could be given to each child attending the celebration.

7. *Las Posadas: A Bilingual Celebration for Christmas*, published by Pauline Books and Media, is an excellent guide which includes the songs and prayers for *Las Posadas*. For those having a larger party, it might be nice to make a big batch of *molletes* cookies, *churros*, *sopaipillas*, and/or *buñuelos*.

Rise Up, Shepherd, and Follow

There's a star in the East on Christmas morn
Rise up shepherds and follow.
It'll show you the place where the child is born.
Rise up shepherds and follow.

Chorus:
Leave your sheep and leave your lambs.
Rise up shepherds and follow.
Leave your ewes and leave your rams.
Rise up shepherds and follow.
Follow, follow, rise up shepherds and follow.
Follow the star of Bethlehem
Rise up shepherds and follow.

African American Spiritual

SIMBANG GABI

(December 16 – 24)

    Simbang Gabi is a Filipino custom which means "Dawn Masses." Imagine crawling out of bed in the early morning darkness to get dressed for a novena of Masses called *Simbang Gabi*. Could you do it? I am not sure I could! In the Philippines since the seventeenth century, many of the workers would rise at three or four in the morning to attend the novena of Masses offered between December 16 and December 24. Permission had been given by the priest to move the Mass time from later in the day to the early morning, so those who labored in the fields and on the sea could attend before going to work. Today if you go to the Philippines you can attend *Simbang Gabi*, and after Mass you will see food vendors waiting to sell you all sorts of yummy rice pastries and tasty drinks such as Spanish hot chocolate, hot coffee, and ginger tea. An air of festivity fills the early morning. The novena of Masses is dedicated to the Blessed Virgin and is considered to be a gift to God by those who attend for the great gift of His Son, soon to be celebrated on Christmas Day.

Filipino Christmas preparations begin very early, around the end of September, with Christmas carols filling the airwaves and star-shaped lanterns called *parols* being hung in the home and around the towns. *Simbang Gabi*, called *Misa de Gallo* in Spanish, signals the beginning of the traditional preparation for the Nativity with families attending the nine Masses and putting out the *belen*, the Christmas crèche in their homes. Many families attend Mass at midnight, called the *Misa de Aguinaldo*, and then have a big meal with much festivity for the *Nochebuena*. The feast of the Epiphany, the celebration of the Three Kings, concludes their Christmas celebrations. Some foods, to name two, *bibingka* (rice flour and egg-based cake) and *puto bumbong* (a purple, sticky rice delicacy steamed, buttered, and sprinkled with brown sugar and coconut), are found only during *Simbang Gabi*, and Filipinos look forward to their availability at this time of year. Many Filipinos when they came to the United States brought their tradition of *Simbang Gabi* to their local parish or diocese. Due to different schedules, the novena of Masses may be offered at times other than the very early morning, but the intent of the novena remains the same, to prepare one's heart for the great gift of Jesus on Christmas day. Here is a recipe for *bibingka*. It has been modified a bit – no charcoal burner to cook it over – but is very tasty. If you do not have time for baking, look to your local Asian grocery for a rice pastry to celebrate and share!

BIBINGKA

(Rice pastry)

Level: Moderate

Here is an authentic *bibingka* recipe, minus the charcoal fire! You may obtain the special ingredients from most Asian stores. Since it is a seasonal treat, call ahead to be sure the ingredients are in stock. Your adventurous shopper and baker will love the fun of preparing it.

PREP: 15 minutes　　　**BAKE: 30-35 minutes**

INGREDIENTS

1 cup rice flour
(plain, not glutinous, from
Asian market)
⅛ teaspoon salt
2 ½ teaspoon baking powder
3 tablespoons unsalted butter
1 cup granulated sugar
1 cup coconut milk
¼ cup fresh milk
1 salted duck egg sliced
(Asian market)
½ cup grated cheese
3 eggs
Pre-cut banana leaf (Asian market)
Shredded coconut

EQUIPMENT

2 small mixing bowls
Electric mixer
Measuring cups
Measuring spoons
1 large spoon
Grater
Wire whisk
Round cake pan

DIRECTIONS: **YIELD:** One cake

1. Preheat oven to 375 degrees Fahrenheit.

2. Combine rice flour, baking powder, and salt. Mix well and set aside.

3. Cream butter, then gradually add sugar while whisking.

4. Add the eggs, then whisk until every ingredient is well incorporated.

5. Gradually add the rice flour mixture to sugar mixture. Continue mixing.

6. Pour coconut milk and fresh milk into the mixture and whisk for 1 to 2 minutes.

7. Arrange the pre-cut banana leaf on the bottom of the cake pan.

8. Pour the mixture into the pan.

9. Bake for 15 minutes.

10. Remove from the oven and top with grated cheese and sliced salted duck egg (do not turn the oven off).

11. Put back in the oven and bake for 15 to 20 minutes or until the top of the *bibingka* turns medium brown.

12. Remove from the oven and let cool.

13. Brush with butter and sprinkle some sugar on top. You can also top this with grated coconut.

14. Serve. Share and enjoy!

(Adapted from the website paniasangpinoy.com)

LESSON FOR SIMBANG GABI

1. Ask the children if anyone is from the Philippines, or if a parent or grandparent is from the Philippines. Explain that the tradition of *Simbang Gabi* is a Filipino custom where families go to Mass early in the morning beginning on December 16 and ending on December 24. They go to Mass for nine days in a row and offer their Masses in honor of the Blessed Mother asking God to help them prepare their hearts for the birth of Jesus. Any prayer or Mass offered nine days in a row is called a novena. Filipino Catholics have a great love of this custom, called *Simbang Gabi*. After Mass, the family stops and buys treats, rice cakes, Spanish hot chocolate, and other pastries. They either eat them at the outdoor markets or take them home and eat them.

2. If *Simbang Gabi* is taking place in your parish or a nearby church, you may wish to take your children to one or more Masses. Often in the U.S. they occur in the evening. Generally there is a program booklet that comes with the Mass and will help the children follow along and participate. There will be lots of delicious treats after Mass, so be sure to drop in with the children and sample them.

3. If there is no *Simbang Gabi* offered nearby, you could take the children to one or more Masses during the nine day novena for the same intention that the Filipinos offer Mass, to help them prepare their hearts for the birth of Jesus. Be sure to explain what you are doing, so they see the connection.

4. If going to Mass during December 16 – December 24 is not possible, why not cut out nine simple red hearts? On each heart write one date, 16, 17, and so on to 24! Each child will have nine hearts. On the front of each heart under the number, have the child write one thing he or she is going to do on that day to prepare his or her heart to celebrate God's gift of Jesus to us. They should have nine hearts with nine different actions. Help them come up with ideas if they get stuck. The actions can be anything from the sublime – a special prayer for Mom or Dad – to the ordinary – picking up their clothes from the floor – to the difficult – sharing a cookie or toy with a brother or sister or classmate.

5. After completing the hearts, you can put each child's in a paper bag with his or her name on it, and beginning on December 16, take the correct heart out each day with its particular activity.

6. Make and bake *bibingka* or buy rice pastries at an Asian supermarket and enjoy the treats.

An Irish Legend

Whoever's born on Christmas
Is favored from the start;
Has laughter and good fortune
And a contented heart;
Is loved by noble company,
Has all that should suffice

But he that dies on Christmas
Goes straight to Paradise.

By Phyllis McGinley

(March 21, 1905 – February 22, 1978)

PARADISE TREE

The Paradise Tree has its origins in medieval Europe and is a central prop of a very popular mystery play called the Paradise Play. The play was performed during Advent, usually on December 24th. It is a retelling of the lives of Adam and Eve, the fall of man and woman, and the promise of the Savior. Originally, the tree was an evergreen with apples hung on it, representing the Garden of Eden. The evergreen symbolized immortality; the apples—often depicted as the fruit of the tree of the knowledge of good and evil—signified the sin of Adam. Later in the fifteenth century white wafers were added to the tree to symbolize Christ, the Sacred Host, the Savior who redeemed man from Adam's sin.

Mystery plays are making a comeback, and it would be fun to make your own Paradise Tree as a prop for a play your students are performing! You may also wish to make a tree to further your students' understanding of salvation history, develop a greater appreciation of the Incarnation, or illustrate the relationship between the Incarnation and the Eucharist.

The Paradise Tree is a forerunner of the Christmas Tree. To learn about its history, read Fr. Francis Weiser's *The Christmas Book* for a more in-depth explanation. The following recipes will allow you to create both an edible and non-edible version of the Paradise Tree for your children to experience.

PARADISE BREAD DOUGH TREE

(Nonedible)

Level: Moderate

PREP: 25 minutes

BAKE: 45 to 60 minutes

INGREDIENTS
4 cups all-purpose flour
1 ½ cups warm water
1 cup salt

EQUIPMENT
Large mixing bowl
Baking sheets
Floured surface
Measuring cups
Apple-shaped cookie cutter

Tree Materials

3-foot terracotta pot filled
with dirt
Artificial evergreen garland
Hammer and nails
Planks of wood
Small saw

Jar or glass 3 ½ inch in diameter
Acrylic paint: red, gold, green, brown
Gold string or yarn
Clear acrylic spray
Small paint brushes

DIRECTIONS:

YIELD: 1 dozen apples & wafers;
1 Paradise Tree

1. Preheat oven to 325 degrees Fahrenheit.

2. Combine flour and salt in large mixing bowl.

3. Make a well in the center of the flour. Mix with hands to achieve thorough blending. Mixture should be moist but not wet.

4. Form dough into a ball. Place on a lightly floured board or surface. Knead for 5 minutes or until smooth.

5. Divide dough into two portions and set one aside.

6. Further divide dough into two portions. Shape into balls.

7. Place one ball on lightly floured surface. Roll out to ¼-inch thickness and cut out apples with cookie cutter. Reroll scraps. You may combine scraps into one last ball of dough for apple cutouts. Roll out. Cut out.

8. With a nail, make a hole for each one for hanging at the base of the apple stem. Be sure it is large enough for yarn to go through but does not crack the stem.

9. Place all bread dough apple cutouts on cookie sheet. Bake at 325 degrees until hard, about 40 minutes.

10. Repeat steps 6-9 with remaining dough. Divide in two. Roll out and cut wafers using the 3 ½-inch jar or glass as cutter. Cutout should be about the size of a communion wafer. With a nail, make a hole for hanging. Reroll scraps and reuse. Repeat steps 7-9 as needed.

11. Remove from oven when hardened and let cool.

12. Paint the apples red with brown stems and green leaves. Paint the wafers white or leave them natural. Paint "IHS" (the name of Jesus from the Greek) with gold paint on each wafer. Let dry, then string. Spray with clear acrylic spray to seal. Allow to dry completely in a well-ventilated room.

TREE

You may buy a real or artificial evergreen tree (small) on which to hang the apples and wafers, or you may make one yourself, following directions below.

1. You will need various pieces of wood, one of each at the following lengths: 3 ½ ft., 3 ft., 2 ft., and 1ft. The longest one should be about 4 inches wide, the others about 3 inches wide.

2. With a pencil draw sharp, arrow-like points on both ends. Points should measure about 3 inches. Saw each piece of wood until each piece has pointed ends.

3. Lay the longest piece of wood flat vertically and place the others horizontally across, with the longer 3-foot piece 12 inches from the lower end, the second 2-foot plank 24 inches from lower end, and the third plank 3 8 inches from the lower end. Nail the 3 pieces of wood securely in place.

4. Place the vertical piece of the Paradise Tree in the 3-foot terra cotta pot filled with dirt. It should go into the pot at a depth of 4 to 6 inches. Be sure the Paradise Tree feels very stable in the pot.

5. Drape artificial evergreen garland over each horizontal piece of wood.

6. Decorate your completed Paradise Tree by hanging the apples and wafers from the branches.

PARADISE COOKIE TREE

(Edible Recipe)

Level: Moderate

The Paradise Tree has undergone various adaptations over the centuries. After the addition of white wafers symbolizing the Sacred Host, other decorations were soon introduced. Cookies in the shapes of angels, flowers, hearts, and bells made from white cookie dough were placed on the tree. These were followed by brown cookie dough decorations in the form of men and women, birds, dogs, and other animals. This recipe may be used with a little adjusting for both light and dark Paradise Tree cookies.

PREP: 20 minutes   **CHILL:** 30 to 45 minutes   **BAKE:** 8 to 10 minutes

INGREDIENTS
4 cups sifted all-purpose flour
4 teaspoons baking powder
½ teaspoon salt
⅓ cup butter or margarine
⅔ cup honey
1 egg
1 teaspoon lemon extract
Cooking spray
⅔ cup molasses (for dark cookies)
1 teaspoon vanilla extract
(for dark cookies)

EQUIPMENT
2 medium-sized mixing bowls
Electric mixer
Measuring cups
Lightly floured surface
Measuring spoons
Rolling pin
Baking sheets
Drinking straw or nail
String for hanging
Glass jar and Cookie cutters

DIRECTIONS:

1. Sift flour, baking powder, and salt into bowl.

2. Beat butter or margarine with brown sugar until fluffy. Beat in honey, egg, and lemon extract.

3. Stir in flour mixture, ⅓ at a time, blending well to make a stiff dough. Chill until firm enough to roll, 30 to 45 minutes.

4. Roll out about ¼ of the dough at a time to a thickness of ⅛ inch on a lightly floured surface. Use a jar to cut out circles for hosts, then use cookie cutters for angels, stars, flowers, bells, and heart shapes.

5. Use a drinking straw or a nail to make a hole at the top of each cookie for hanging.

6. Place cookies 1 inch apart on greased cookie sheet. Bake at 350 degrees Fahrenheit for 8 minutes until firm.

7. Cool and then string for hanging.

Variation: For the dark cookies use the same directions and ingredients, except for the honey substitute ⅔ cup molasses, and for the lemon extract substitute 1 teaspoon vanilla extract, and cut the shapes recommended for the dark dough—men and women, birds, dogs, and other animals.

CHRISTMAS CRÈCHE

St. Francis of Assisi loved the Nativity of Jesus so much that he desired to recreate the scene for himself and the people of Greccio, Italy. In his biography of St. Francis, Thomas de Celano quotes the saint as saying to a friend: "If you desire that we should celebrate this year's Christmas together at Greccio, go quickly and prepare what I tell you; for I want to enact the memory of the Infant who was born at Bethlehem, and how He was deprived of all the comforts babies enjoy; how He was bedded in the manger on hay, between an ass and an ox. For once I want to see all this with my own eyes." St. Francis' friend prepared everything as requested.

On Christmas Eve, in the year 1223, the people of Greccio assembled with candles and torches to see the Nativity of Jesus recreated before their very eyes. All were moved by what they saw, but none more than St. Francis himself, who was overcome by the scene of God's tender love. Mass was offered at midnight, and together all in Greccio raised their minds and hearts to God in praise. Since then Christians throughout the world have been inspired to recreate the scene of Our Savior's birth.

It is deeply satisfying to make your own Christmas crèche, one you and your children can keep for many years. We use our ever- favorite bread dough recipe to make ours. I have always thought that making a crèche is a wonderfully creative Advent project for students of all ages. The children enjoy bringing the Nativity scene to life with their own hands, and how marvelous for all to see the great variety of talent in our young people!

Artists from Naples, Italy, are known for creating elaborate crèche scenes with a personal touch. Not only do they depict Jesus, the Holy Family, the shepherds, and wise men, but they recreate the entire Nativity as though it happened in their own towns and villages, with all of the local people present. If you would like to see an exquisite example of a Baroque Neapolitan crèche, make a visit to the Metropolitan Museum of Art in New York City during the Advent and Christmas Seasons. There on display you will see a truly magnificent crèche scene, consisting of more than two hundred figures.

BREAD DOUGH CHRISTMAS CRÈCHE

To make the bread dough, follow the recipe for the Bread Dough Advent Wreath. After you have prepared the dough, continue with the directions which follow.

DIRECTIONS: **YIELD:** many figures

1. Decide which figures you want to make for your crèche. Jesus, Mary, and Joseph are the main figures. You can keep it simple, or you may choose to make the angels, shepherds, wise men, as well as people from your family, neighborhood, school, church, etc.

2. Take a small amount of the bread dough and form it into the shape of a ball. Work the bread dough to see how it feels and responds. If it is too dry to mold, sprinkle with a few drops of water and blend well. If the dough is too sticky, add a small amount of flour and work it in.

3. Form the first ball into a figure two or three inches high. This is the body of your figure. It should look like an inverted letter "U," a bit bigger on the bottom and smaller on the top.

4. Take a smaller piece of dough and shape into a round ball for the head. Attach to the body by slightly moistening the base of the head and the top of the body with egg yolk or a dab of white glue.

5. Take smaller pieces of dough to roll into small ropes. These will be the arms. Attach the arms the same way as the head: attach one end of each arm to the shoulder areas of your figure, and bring the other ends around to the front as if in prayer. For your figures of the shepherds or St. Joseph, you may want to roll a piece of dough for the shepherd's crook and place it on the side of the figure before you attach the arm. Attach the arm around the crook to hold it in place.

6. Now you can either make a shepherd's headdress or veil by rolling out a small piece of dough into a flat rectangle. Place on the head using a bit of yolk and fashion the headdress so it hangs properly. (See drawings for help.)

7. You may use small pieces of dough for beards on the men, wings on the angels, etc.

8. Be sure your figures are of the same size and shape for baking purposes.

9. The baby Jesus may be formed by rolling a piece of dough in the shape of a small cigar. Roll another piece for the infant head and attach. The infant will be placed in a small manger.

10. For the manger, take a piece of dough the size of a small fist. Hollow out the inside so it can accommodate the infant you made. You can shape the dough to resemble a basket or add legs to the manger. Be sure the figure of the infant Jesus can fit in the manger after baking. Bake at 325 degrees Fahrenheit until all figures are hard and dry, but not overly browned.

11. Paint faces, clothes, and hair on the well-dried figures and then seal with clear acrylic spray. Be sure to spray in a well-ventilated area, preferably out of doors. You may want to spread evergreen branches or obtain palm trees from a craft store to complete your crèche scene.

12. When putting away your crèche figures at the end of the Christmas Season, store in plastic baggies in a cool, dry place.

Blessing for the Crèche

Lord, bless all who look upon this crèche. May it remind us of the humble birth of Jesus, and raise up our thoughts to Him, who is God-with-us and Savior of all, and who lives and reigns forever and ever. Amen.

SAMPLE FIGURE FOR
BREAD DOUGH CRÈCHE

SAMPLE FIGURE FOR BREAD DOUGH CRÈCHE

CHOCOLATE CRÈCHE
Level: Easy

In the last week before school closes for Christmas vacation, or at home right up to Christmas Eve, this pre-Christmas activity will keep the children focused on the birth of Jesus and busily engaged. The time involved in making the candy crèches is minimal, and they may be displayed and/or given as gifts. For a large group of children, twenty–five or more, you will want many molds* and a couple of microwaves. You might want to work in groups of five and schedule different groups throughout the day, or you may spread the activity out over a few days.

The crèche scenes are made by pouring heated chocolate melts into plastic molds. The chocolate sets until it is firm and then is unmolded. The finished pieces are then assembled into a crèche scene. If you use white chocolate melts, you may paint them with candy color. Many of the inexpensive plastic molds may be used for molding butter or wax, also.

PREP: 2 min. melting,   **CHILL:** 20 min. in refrigerator or or less 5 min. in freezer   **UNMOLD:** 1-2 min.

INGREDIENTS
1-lb. bag white chocolate candy melts,
or chocolate candy melts,
and colored candy melts for painting white chocolate melts

*molds are inexpensive

EQUIPMENT
Nativity molds (purchase at party or craft store, or order at Amazon on-line; see Resource section)
Small paint brushes for candy
Microwave or double boiler
Microwave-safe bowls for melting
Large spoon for stirring
Smaller plastic spoons
Measuring cups

DIRECTIONS: YIELD: Varies according to size of molds

1. Melt about 1 cup of chocolate candy melts in microwavable bowl on high for 30 seconds. Remove from microwave and stir. If solid bits of chocolate remain, return to microwave and heat for 15 seconds. Remove from heat and stir until chocolate pieces are melted. If any pieces remain, return to microwave and heat for 10 seconds. Repeat until melted. **It is important not to burn the chocolate.** Microwaves vary, so it is better to err on too little time and repeat the process, checking often. Carefully pour out the melted chocolate, guiding it with a spoon into your molds. Molds should be filled completely. Remaining chocolate can be reheated and reused.

2. Gently tap the mold to release air bubbles. You will see the bubbles rise to the surface and evaporate. Tap until no air bubbles remain.

3. Place molds in the refrigerator. The duration of time depends on the size and depth of the mold. Check every 5 minutes. You may place molds in the freezer, but unless carefully watched, the chocolate has a tendency to crack when unmolded.

4. Remove chocolate from mold by gently tapping it.

5. To paint white crèche figures, heat some extra chocolate, add coloring, blend well, and paint. Be sure to use small, clean paint brushes. You can purchase them in a craft store. ***Warning: do not use any coloring that is water-based or that needs water. Water ruins chocolate.**

6. When completed, your crèche may be displayed, given as a gift, and, of course, eventually eaten!

7. You may store it in a plastic freezer bag in the freezer if you don't eat it right away.

BREAD DOUGH CHRISTMAS ORNAMENTS
Level: Easy

 This is a very enjoyable activity for children ages eight and older.* In the classroom, it requires a block of time which varies, depending on the ratio of adults to children. If parents make the dough ahead of time at home, children in a classroom can roll it out on their desks and cut out the designs using cookie cutters. The ornaments are baked for one hour, a little less if rolled thin. Painting the ornaments may be done another day; it takes about twenty minutes to paint three to five ornaments. Time involved in preparing the environment and cleaning up afterwards is additional. Use the recipe from the Bread Dough Advent Wreath. When the dough is prepared, continue with the following directions.

DIRECTIONS:

1. Separate large ball of dough into two equal size balls.

2. Roll one ball out into large circle of ¼ inch thickness.

3. Take cookie cutters and cut out shapes, beginning on the outer edges of the dough. Follow the circle, finishing by cutting out shapes in the interior of the circle. Poke a hole in each cutout with a nail for hanging. Gently place the ornaments on a baking sheet(s).

4. Repeat steps 1 through 3 with second ball of dough.

5. Heat oven to 325 degrees Fahrenheit. Bake ornaments for 35 to 40 minutes or until hard and dry.

6. Remove from oven. Cool. Remove from baking tray. Place on newspapers for painting. Paint. Let dry.

7. In a well-ventilated room spray the ornaments with clear acrylic spray. Spray one side. Let dry. Spray reverse side, taking care not to let the newspaper stick to your ornament.

8. Thread yarn through each ornament and tie a knot. Hang the ornaments on the tree or give them as gifts. To store, place in a plastic bag in a cool, dry place.

*Younger children love painting these ornaments.

CHRISTMAS SEASON

Vigil of Christmas—Baptism of the Lord

December 24—January 9

Unto Us A Child Is Born

Unto us a child is born, unto us a Son is given, and the government shall be upon His shoulder; and His name shall be called Wonderful, Counsellor, the Mighty God, the Everlasting Father, the Prince of Peace. (Isaiah 9:6)

chorus to *the Messiah* by George Frideric Handel
(February 23, 1685 – April 14, 1759)

NATIVITY OF THE LORD

Solemnity, December 25

Is December 25th the actual day of Jesus' birth? The answer may surprise you— no one really knows! All we know for sure is that for centuries, since about 325 AD, Christians from around the world have celebrated December 25th as the birthday of the Lord.

In the early Church after Christ's death, His birth was celebrated by many on the Feast of the Epiphany, sometimes called the Manifestation of the Lord. Some Catholics still exchange gifts on this feast day. After the last great persecution by the Romans, in about 325 AD, the Church set aside December 25th as the birthday of Jesus. Many unofficial explanations are given as to why this date was chosen. Some Fathers of the Church held that the date was known from the official Roman census taken at the time of Christ's birth. However, no record of that census exists. Others maintained that Jesus had to be born at the beginning of a new solar cycle, because that is what the Bible states. Neither theory could be substantiated.

Today, most scholars believe that the early Church chose December 25th because the date was already an auspicious one for Rome, which, at the time, ruled much of the then-known world. The Romans honored their sun god, Sol Invictus, on that date, while the popular Mithras cult also held great celebrations on December 25th for the birthday of the sun. To guide newly converted Christians away from the pagan worship of the sun and to the worship and celebration of the birthday of the Son of God, the Church chose the date of December 25th.

In the United States and throughout much of the world, birthday celebrations are very special. The day of one's birth is annually recalled by the family with gifts, cake or festive foods, and perhaps a party including friends. How fitting then to have a birthday cake either at home, CCD class, or in the school classroom to celebrate the greatest birth of all—God becoming man! Honoring Jesus' birthday with a cake is an effective way to teach children the awesome significance of Christmas Day. It helps to move the spotlight off the children receiving gifts and on to the reason behind the gift giving: God's gift to us—Jesus.

Many of the recipes that follow have a culinary history associated with Christmas and enrich not only our palates but our understanding of Catholic culture through the ages. Consult the Resource and Bibliography sections in the back of this book for more information.

HAPPY BIRTHDAY CAKE

For Baby Jesus

Level: Easy

PREP: 10 minutes   **BAKE:** 30 minutes   **DECORATE:** 10 minutes

INGREDIENTS	EQUIPMENT
1 cake mix (your favorite)	Large mixing bowl
Eggs (follow directions on box)	Electric mixer
Vegetable oil or butter	Measuring cups
(follow directions on box)	Tooth picks
⅛ cup of all-purpose flour	Two 9-inch round cake pans
Water	Wire racks
Baking spray	

Frosting/Decorations*	
½ cup butter or	Medium mixing bowl
margarine (1 stick)	Electric mixer
⅔ cup Hershey's cocoa	Small saucepan or micro-
3 cups confectioners' sugar	wavable bowl
⅓ cup milk	Measuring spoons
1 teaspoon vanilla	Spoon for scraping
	Knife for spreading

Filling*	
1 pint heavy whipping cream	Medium mixing bowl
1 teaspoon vanilla	Electric mixer
Sugar if desired	Spoon for scraping
Hershey's Chocolate Kisses®	Birthday candles
(Christmas-colored foil-wrapped)	

DIRECTIONS:

1. Follow the directions on back of cake box, but add one more egg and ⅛ cup of all-purpose flour. This makes the cake a little firmer and adds height. (Disregard this addition if you are making an Angel Food cake.)

2. Set oven temperature 25 degrees Fahrenheit less than stated on the box. This eliminates the hump that you sometimes see on the top of a cake. Spray pans with floured cake spray. Then divide cake batter and fill each cake pan evenly. Place in oven and bake.

3. Check for doneness by inserting a wooden toothpick into the center of the cake. If the toothpick comes out clean, the cake is done. Otherwise, add a few minutes to the baking time and check back until toothpick comes out clean.

4. When done, remove from oven. Cool for ten minutes and then remove from pan to a rack. Finish cooling. While cake is baking, make whipped cream filling or another favorite.

5. If your mixing bowl is metal, put in the freezer for a few minutes before you whip the cream.

6. Place cream in mixing bowl. Beat on high for a couple of minutes then add 1 teaspoon of vanilla. If desired add ¼ cup of confectioners' sugar or granulated sugar. Continue beating until firm peaks are formed. Be careful not to beat too long, or the cream will separate into chunks or curds. Put whipped cream in refrigerator until ready to decorate.

7. For Frosting – melt butter or margarine in a small saucepan on stove or in the microwave. Remove as soon as it is melted. Pour into mixing bowl. Stir cocoa into melted butter.

8. Alternately add confectioners' sugar and milk, beating with electric mixer until spreading consistency. Add additional milk if needed. Stir in vanilla. Makes two cups of frosting.

9. To decorate, assemble the cake, whipped cream, frosting, birthday candles & Hershey's Kisses®. You may buy a cake to frost, and purchase frosting and filling if time is a consideration.

10. Let the children take turns frosting the cake, applying the whipped cream, arranging the Christmas-colored foiled candies, and putting on the candles. How many candles you put on the cake is up to you. One idea is to place a candle for every century since Jesus' birth.

11. Since this is a two-layer cake, have one child put some frosting on the first layer. A second child can put on the whipped cream.* Place the second layer on top carefully. Then let another child frost the top of the cake – make it nice and generous and luscious. Your next child helper can put the whipped cream in the center on top of the frosting and spread it, but make sure not to cover the entire top – about ¾ of an inside circle.

12. Give all the remaining children Hershey's Kisses® and candles. One at a time, have them put on the kisses and candles. Voila! Your birthday cake for Baby Jesus is complete!

"HAPPY BIRTHDAY BABY JESUS"

*Be careful with the whipped cream filling between the first and second layers. We once had the top layer slide right off as my son took it downstairs to store in our second refrigerator until dinnertime. It was a rather modest birthday cake that year! However, that minor setback has not prevented us from using whipped cream. We are just a bit more careful when carrying the cake!

*Cupcakes are perfect if you prefer the smaller size for home or classroom. You can make a special cupcake for Baby Jesus. It should be fancier than all the rest!

Some bakers prefer other toppings. One suggestion is crushed candy canes instead of kisses.

A LESSON TO CELEBRATE
THE SAVIOR'S BIRTH

The focus of this lesson is the celebration of the Incarnation scaled down to a child's level. Our Lord told us that it is to such as these (children) that the kingdom of heaven belongs (see Luke 18:16).

1. Read the Gospel account of the birth of Our Lord (Luke 2:1–20). Remind the children that the Jewish people had been waiting a long time for the Savior to come. Finally, with the birth of Jesus, God fulfilled His promise. Emphasize that God keeps His promises and that He kept it in a wonderful way: He sent His own Son to us.

2. Place the figure of the baby Jesus in the Nativity scene you have set up.

3. Have the children decorate a birthday cake to celebrate the anniversary of His birth. We have included a recipe to make a cake from a mix, or you may buy a plain cake and decorate it, or make your own from scratch.

4. To decorate the cake you will need frosting, whipped cream or some other filling, Hershey's Kisses® —green, red, and silver—and birthday candles (perhaps one for each century).

5. Have an adult light the candles; all present can gather around the cake to sing "Happy Birthday" to Jesus. Cut the cake and enjoy.

6. You may wish to end the lesson with giving the children some small gift—a prayer card with a picture of the Nativity on the front, or a small Nativity scene, or some other item of your choosing.

MEXICAN WEDDING COOKIES
Level: Moderate

*Nuts

This cookie is found at special celebrations in Mexico— weddings, birthdays, Christmas, and more. It is not a recipe to make with young children; it would be more appropriate with bakers at least nine and older. I must say, these cookies are among the best I have ever eaten, and this recipe is certainly one to save for the greatest of feasts! It is taken from Nancy Baggett's *International Cookie Cook Book*. Nancy Baggett is the queen of cookie and dessert bakers, in my opinion. Please try this recipe and see if you don't agree.

PREP: 30 minutes   **BAKE:** 8 to 10 minutes

INGREDIENTS   **EQUIPMENT**
1 ½ cups coarsely   Baking pans
chopped pecans   Large mixing spoon
1 ½ cups unsalted butter,   Food processor or blender
slightly softened   Large mixing bowl
¼ teaspoon salt   Electric mixer
⅔ cup powdered sugar   Wire racks
2 teaspoons vanilla
3 cups all-purpose flour
Baking spray or margarine for greasing sheets
Decoration
½ to ⅔ cups powdered sugar

DIRECTIONS: **YIELD:** 50 cookies

1. Preheat the oven to 325 degrees Fahrenheit.

2. Spread the pecans in a large baking pan. Place in the oven and toast, stirring frequently, for 8 to 10 minutes, or until fragrant and very lightly tinged with brown. Remove from the oven and set aside until cooled completely.

3. Grind the pecans to a powder using a nut grinder, food processor, or blender.

4. Reset oven temperature to 350 degrees F. Grease several baking sheets and set aside.

5. Place the butter and salt in a large mixing bowl and beat with electric mixer on medium speed until light and fluffy. Add ⅔ cup powdered sugar and vanilla and continue beating until very fluffy and smooth. Beat in cooled ground pecans. Gradually beat in flour. If the mixer motor begins to labor, stir in last of the flour by hand.

6. Pull off dough pieces and roll between the palms into 1 ¼-inch balls. Space them about 2 inches apart on baking sheets. Flatten balls slightly with the heel of the hand to form 1½- inch discs.

7. Place in the upper third of the oven and bake 10 to 12 minutes, or until cookies are just faintly tinged with brown at the edges and still pale in the centers.

8. Remove baking sheets from oven and let stand about 5 minutes. Using a spatula, gently transfer cookies to wire racks and let stand until cooled slightly.

9. Sift powdered sugar generously over the cookies and let them stand until cooled completely.

10. Store cookies in an airtight container for up to a week. For best appearance, add an additional light sifting of powdered sugar shortly before serving. The cookies may also be frozen before sprinkling with powdered sugar, then thawed completely and decorated before serving.

CHRISTMAS SUGAR COOKIES

Christmas is the season to pull out all the stops when it comes to decorating cookies. The recipe found in the section on the Feast of the Immaculate Conception is one of the best sugar cookie recipes around and makes five dozen cookies. Use your favorite Christmas cookie cutters, then let your imagination go wild as you frost and decorate with cut-up cherries, nuts, chocolate bits, sprinkles, white chocolate, craisins®, and more. Dip paper-thin cookies in melted chocolate, or ice thickly-rolled favorite cutouts with a scrumptious frosting recipe. Don't forget to add coconut, toasted or plain, to some of the cookies. Now is the time to celebrate with all the abundance nature gives us!

Hodie Christus natus est!

KOURAMBIEDES

(Butter Cookies)

Level: Moderate

Here is a butter cookie whose symbolism is sure to enchant some young bakers. The Greeks make this cookie for weddings, anniversaries, and special celebrations. At Christmastime you will find the cookie spiked with a whole clove as a reminder of the gift of spices brought to the Christ child by the Magi. You may want to save this cookie for an Epiphany party.

PREP: 20 minutes

BAKE: 12 to 15 minutes

INGREDIENTS

1 cup unsalted butter, softened
½ cup confectioners' sugar
1 egg yolk
2 teaspoon anise-flavored extract
½ teaspoon almond extract
2 cups all-purpose flour
48 whole cloves

Decoration

Confectioners' sugar

EQUIPMENT

Large mixing bowl
Measuring cups
Measuring spoons
Baking sheets
Wire racks

DIRECTIONS: **YIELD:** 48 cookies

1. Cream butter, ½ cup confectioners' sugar, the egg yolk, anise-flavored and almond extracts until light and fluffy; stir in flour.

2. Shape the dough by teaspoonfuls into round balls. Place about 1 inch apart on ungreased baking sheet. Flatten cookie in middle and spike center of cookie with a clove.

3. Bake at 350 degrees Fahrenheit for 12 to 15 minutes or until light brown on the bottom.

4. Sprinkle with confectioners' sugar while hot. Cool on wire racks.

MINCEMEAT PIE

Level: Easy

Until I was ten years old, my family shared a house with my grandmother in Vermont. Gram was a cookie and pie baker, and a few times a year she would make donuts. Mincemeat pie was one of her favorites to bake during the colder months. I grew up loving mincemeat, but it wasn't until I was much older that I learned the very interesting Catholic history behind the pie.

Bakers in England concocted the Christmas mince pie when the crusaders returned from the Holy Land with spices native to Our Lord's birthplace. They fashioned the pie served at Christmastime into a manger, and the oblong-shaped pie sometimes had an indention in the top crust in which a figure of the baby Jesus was placed. The mince pie became a devotional device and a special food to celebrate the birth of Christ.

During the Reformation (1517 to 1648), the Puritans reacted strongly against the devotional elements of the mince pie and banned it altogether from Christmas celebrations. To eat the mince pie was, in their minds, to succumb to idolatry, superstition, and popish observance—it was an abomination! But both Catholics and Anglicans defended the eating of the mince pie. When the Puritans came to power in the seventeenth century, the mince pie was legally banned. Forbidden or not, the English population continued eating the pie. When the monarchy was restored in 1660, the legal ban was removed and the mince pie resumed its place as center attraction at the English Christmas table. In his *Christmas Book,* Fr. Weiser reminds us that "ironically enough, the Puritans also won their victory." The practice of shaping the pie in the form of a manger was gone forever, except as an occasional curiosity. The mincemeat pie came to New England in circular form, and from there made its way to other parts of the country.

When making the mince pie at Christmas, why not shape it in the form of a manger as our Catholic ancestors did so long ago?

PIE FILLING

PREP: 20 minutes   **BAKE:** 50 minutes

INGREDIENTS
1 jar or box of mincemeat
Water
2 prepared pie crusts or recipe below

EQUIPMENT
Medium-sized saucepan
Large spoon

Medium-sized mixing bowl

PIE CRUST

INGREDIENTS
2 cups all-purpose flour
½ teaspoon salt
1 ½ sticks cold butter
½ cup ice water

EQUIPMENT
Measuring cups & spoons
Pastry cutter
Pastry cutter
Loaf pan or 9-inch pie plate
Medium-sized mixing bowl
Rolling pin
Lightly floured surface

DIRECTIONS: **YIELD:** 1 pie

1. Combine flour and salt in a mixing bowl. Cut in butter with pastry cutter until the mixture resembles coarse meal.

2. Make a well and add the water slowly. Mix briefly with fork. Add another tablespoon or two if the mixture is too dry.

3. Divide the dough into two balls, ⅓ and ⅔ size of dough. Wrap in plastic wrap and chill for ½ hour. Continue with pie filling.

Assemble Crust & Pie Filling

1. Follow directions on the container of mincemeat.

2. Remove pie crust dough from refrigerator or follow directions for a prepared crust.

3. Roll larger ball of dough into the oblong shape.

4. Place rolled pie crust in a loaf pan with edges rising up 2 ½ inches.

5. Spoon in mincemeat filling. Be sure filling does not extend over the edges.

6. Roll remainder of pie crust to cover the top of the filling. Place on top of filling and pinch the top and bottom crust edges together with your fingers or a crust edging tool. Make an indention for the figure of the baby Jesus. Prick some holes for air to escape while baking. You can make a design for the air holes—holly leaves or candles would be nice!

7. Bake in preheated 400 degrees Fahrenheit oven for 50 minutes, or according to package directions. Crust should be lightly browned and filling bubbling.

8. Remove from oven. Let cool and enjoy.

STOLLEN

(German Christmas Bread)

Level: Challenging

*Nuts

This traditional Christmas bread takes its shape from the swaddling clothes placed on Jesus by his mother Mary (Luke 2:7). The Germans have made *stollen* since the Middle Ages. If you prefer to buy one, look for one that shows the seams. If you bake one, be sure to fold the dough seam side up and allow for ample room on the baking sheet so the effect of the swaddling clothes is seen.

PREP: 30 minutes   **RISE:** 1 ½ hours   **BAKE:** 20 to 25 minutes
RISE: 1 hour

INGREDIENTS

½ cup diced citron

½ cup raisins or currants

¼ cup candied diced orange peel

¼ cup brandy, rum, or fruit juice

1 package active dry yeast

¼ cup warm water
(105 – 115 degrees)

½ cup lukewarm milk
(scalded, then cooled)

½ cup (1 stick) butter or
margarine, softened

½ cup granulated sugar

½ teaspoon salt

¼ teaspoon ground nutmeg

3 eggs

EQUIPMENT

Small mixing bowl

Measuring cups & spoons

Large spoon

Strainer

Large mixing bowl

Electric mixer

Lightly floured surface

Greased mixing bowl

Greased baking sheet

Small pastry brush

Small saucepan

4—4 ½ cups all-purpose flour

½ cup chopped, blanched almonds

1 tablespoon finely shredded lemon peel

2 tablespoons butter or margarine, melted

Confectioners' sugar

DIRECTIONS: **YIELD:** 2 loaves

1. Mix citron, raisins, orange peel, and brandy; let stand at least 1 hour. Drain; reserve brandy.

2. Dissolve yeast in warm water in large bowl. Stir in reserved brandy, the milk, ½ cup butter, the granulated sugar, salt, nutmeg, eggs, and 2 cups of flour. Beat until smooth.

3. Stir in brandied fruit mixture, almonds, lemon peel, and enough remaining flour to make dough easy to handle.

4. Turn dough onto a lightly floured surface and knead until smooth and elastic, about 5 minutes.

5. Place dough in a greased mixing bowl; turn greased side up. Cover. Let rise in a warm place until double, about 1 ½ hours. (Dough is ready if indentation remains when touched.)

6. Punch down dough; divide in half. Press one half into an oval shape, about 10 x 7 inches. Brush with melted butter. Fold lengthwise in half and press folded edges firmly. Place *stollen* on greased cookie sheet. Repeat with remaining dough.

7. Cover and let rise until double, 45 to 60 minutes.

8. Brush with melted butter. Heat oven to 375 degrees Fahrenheit. Bake until golden brown, 20 to 25 minutes. Remove from oven. Let cool.

9. Brush with melted butter and sprinkle with confectioners' sugar.

When the angels went away from them into heaven, the shepherds said to one another, "Let us go over to Bethlehem and see this thing that has happened, which the Lord has made known to us." And they went with haste, and found Mary and Joseph, and the baby lying in a manger. (Luke 2:15-16)

FEAST OF THE HOLY FAMILY

Sunday within the Octave of Christmas

During Advent many of our celebrations focus on honoring the saints, rejoicing in their victories and virtues, while asking for their help. On the Feast of the Holy Family which occurs during the Christmas Season, we honor Jesus, Mary, and Joseph—the holiest of families and the model for all family life. In the encyclical *The Role of the Christian Family in the Modern World*, the family is referred to as the "domestic church," the basic building block of the hierarchical Church. It is in the home that children first receive the gift of faith. Today, let us celebrate the gifts of the Holy Family, our own families, and our Catholic faith. Any number of foods can be used to celebrate this feast day. Here is a baking project that is easy and allows for great creativity in decorating.

LOLLIPOP COOKIES

Level: Easy

PREP: 15 minutes   **BAKE:** 7 to11 minutes   **DECORATE:** 15 minutes

INGREDIENTS
2 packages refrigerated
sugar cookie dough
1 cup all-purpose flour
40 lollipop sticks or
ice cream sticks
Colored frostings, glazes,
candies, sprinkles, colored
sugars, and jimmies
Baking spray

EQUIPMENT
Floured surface
Rolling pin
Cookie cutters
Baking sheets
Wire racks

DIRECTIONS: YIELD: 40 cookies

1. Remove dough from one wrapper. Sprinkle dough lightly with flour.

2. Cut dough in half, reserve half; place remaining dough back in refrigerator.

3. Roll reserved dough on floured surface to ⅛ inch. With cookie cutters cut out a variety of Christmas shapes—baby Jesus, Mary, Joseph, stars, angels, shepherds, lambs, Christmas trees, bells, bears— everything your family enjoys using to celebrate the family: Jesus' and yours!

4. Insert lollipop or ice cream sticks so that the tips are imbedded in the cookies. Place on sprayed/greased baking sheets.

5. Heat oven to 350 degrees Fahrenheit and bake cookies 7 to 11 minutes or until lightly browned. Cool on racks.

6. Repeat steps 3-5 with remaining dough.

7. Decorate with frostings, sugars, and candies, as desired.

LESSON ON THE HOLY FAMILY

Jesus, Mary, and Joseph were a family, and they lived as all families do— eating, working, playing, praying, and sleeping. What made their family holy? Jesus, who is God, was their Son, and Mary and Joseph lived out their family life by following the plan God had designed for their family. They are the model for all families because they followed God's Will in all things.

Read Luke 2:22-35. Summarize: Mary and Joseph with Jesus go to the Temple to present Him to the Lord. While there, a holy man, Simeon, sees the Child and recognizes Him as the Savior. Simeon takes the baby Jesus in his arms (Luke 2:29-32). He blesses the Holy Family, and then he prophesied to Mary that Jesus will be the downfall and the rise of many, and that a sword will pierce Mary's heart. Joseph, Mary, and Jesus accept the prophecy and live out their lives according to God's Will (Luke 2:39-40). Let us honor the example of the Holy Family and ask them to help our families follow God's Will for us.

We confess the holy virgin to be the mother of God because God the Word took flesh and became man and from his very conception united to himself the temple he took from her. (Council of Ephesus, 431)

SOLEMNITY OF MARY, MOTHER OF GOD

January 1

In the United States, as well as in all countries that follow the Gregorian calendar, January 1 is the first day of the New Year. The evening before the New Year is often spent partying, and there are many secular traditions associated with New Year's Eve.

The celebration of the Solemnity of Mary on January 1 is relatively new, instituted in 1970. It resulted from the revision of the General Roman Calendar under Pope Paul VI. There are not a great many customs associated yet with the Solemnity of Mary, but it is a solemn feast which indicates its significance. The question is: how do we honor Mary under this title? The Church answers in part by observing the day as a holy day of obligation; we honor Mary first and foremost by going to Mass. Many people then relax on this day after all the Christmas festivities. If you decide you want to try something new, the following is an adaptation of a recipe taken from *A Continual Feast* by Evelyn Birge Vitz. It is based on a custom from England, in which Coventry God-Cakes were given to godchildren on New Year's Day. You may want to bake them with your family and take some to your godchildren if they are close by.

COVENTRY GOD-CAKES
Level: Easy

PREP: 10 minutes   **BAKE:** 20 - 25 minutes

INGREDIENTS
Store-bought fillings: ,
lemon, cream
raspberry or strawberry
Store-bought puff pastry shells
Whipped cream or sprinkles for garnish

EQUIPMENT
Several plastic teaspoons
Baking sheets
Fork or Pastry sealer

DIRECTIONS: **YIELD:** 6 filled pastry puffs

1. Preheat oven to 400 degrees Fahrenheit. Bake puff pastry shells according to the directions on the package. Remove from oven when done. Cool.

2. Remove top of shells and scoop out soft pastry inside.

3. Fill with your favorite filling.

4. Top with whipped cream or colored sprinkles.

CAKE POPS FOR MARY

Level: Easy

Cake pops are very fashionable. They are delectable and almost melt in your mouth. They can be, when carefully decorated, beautiful, even elegant. While they do not "own" a page in Catholic food history, I am proposing them for inclusion! Whenever a cook or baker prepares a food for celebration, that food may become part of the Catholic cultural tradition, particularly if used repeatedly to celebrate a feast day. I am betting cake pops are here to stay. I can think of few easier, more luscious, or more appealing treats for children to make for Mary, with Mom's help, than the delectable cake pops.

PREP: 10 minutes   **BAKE:** about 38 minutes   **CHILL:** 2 hours **DECORATE:**
20 minutes

INGREDIENTS

1 cake mix (any but angel
food, may use
Gluten-free cake mix)
Eggs (follow directions on box)
Oil or butter
(follow directions on box)
Water
Baking spray (may use floured
spray or ¼ cup dusting flour)
Frosting
1 can frosting (your preference)
Large spoon
36 4- inch lollipop sticks

EQUIPMENT

Large mixing bowl
Electric mixer
Measuring cups
9 x 13-inch pan
Wire racks
Large spoon

Large mixing bowl

Decorations

Chocolate melts (various colors)   Microwavable bowls
Colored sugars, jimmies, sprinkles   Plastic spoons and knives

DIRECTIONS: YIELD: 36 cake pops

1. Prepare cake mix according to the directions on the box.

2. Set oven at 350 degrees Fahrenheit or as directions suggest.

3. Spray rectangular 9 x 13-inch pan, glass or aluminum, and dust with flour if necessary.

4. Spoon cake mix into prepared pan. Place in oven and bake according to directions.

5. Test to determine doneness by inserting a toothpick or sharp knife. If toothpick comes out clean,   cake is done. Otherwise continue baking for a few more minutes. Do not over or under bake.

6. Remove cake from oven and let cool in pan on wire rack.

7. When cool, remove cake in chunks from pan and completely crumble in clean mixing bowl. Be sure to crumble entire cake so that there are not any lumps.

8. Add about ½ - ⅔ cup of prepared frosting into crumbled cake and mix well. Be sure the cake is moist enough to be rolled into balls but not wet.

9. Prepare a large cookie sheet or rectangular cake pan by lining it with aluminum foil, wax paper, or plastic wrap.

10. Roll cake mixture into 1-inch balls and place a 4-inch lollipop stick in each one. Place on prepared cookie sheet and then freeze for two hours or until hard.

DECORATE

1. Remove cake pops from freezer when hard.

2. Melt candy melts, whatever colors and flavors that complement your cake pops in a microwavable dish. Start with about one cup of melts. Microwave for 45 second on high. Stir. Microwave for another 15 seconds and stir. When the chocolate is a liquid, the melts are ready for dipping. Be careful not to overcook the melts.

3. Take one cake pop and dip it into the melts, turning it around so the entire pop is covered. You can use a plastic spoon or knife to be sure it is entirely covered. Gradually lift it out of the melts and place on prepared sheet.

4. Decorate with sprinkles, sugars or jimmies immediately, before chocolate hardens. Repeat with all the frozen cake pops until all are decorated, then place in the refrigerator until you are ready to eat them. They present very well and are scrumptious. Both regular cake mixes and gluten-free cake mixes do very well with this recipe. Try not to eat too many!

LESSON FOR THE SOLEMNITY OF MARY, THE MOTHER OF GOD

The Solemnity of Mary falls during the Christmas Season. You may be teaching the children about Mary's great title, Mother of God (*Theotokos*), at some other time of the year. Whenever you teach this great truth, here are some vital points to share:

1. Remind the children that God created Mary and gave her many special gifts because she was to be the mother of His Son, Jesus.

2. The Immaculate Conception was a special gift that God gave Mary which preserved her from Original Sin. Another beautiful gift is her title: Mother of God.

3. Explain to the children that Mary is Jesus' mother—really and truly. Jesus is the Second Person of the Blessed Trinity; yet, from the moment Jesus was conceived in Mary's womb by the power of the Holy Spirit, He was her son. When Jesus became man, Mary became mother of Jesus who is God. We celebrate Mary's special role on January 1 by proclaiming her great title, Mother of God, and going to Mass in her honor.

4. Make Coventry God-Cakes, cake pops for Mary, or buy a favorite treat and enjoy it with family and friends. Thank Jesus for giving us the gift of His Blessed Mother and thank Mary for being the *Theotokos*, "the God-bearer," the mother who brought the God/man to us.

O man, know then that God becomes flesh

And where did this incarnation take place?

The body of a Holy Virgin!

Let us, too, burst forth with voice of joy.

Let us celebrate the mystery of the Salvation of the whole world,

The birthday of mankind.

Today the blame of Adam is revoked.

No longer: "You are dust, and to us dust you will return";

But, closely united to the celestial world,

You will be lifted even into Heaven.

No longer: in pain will you bear sons;

But, blessed is the one who has borne Emmanuel

And blessed is the womb that nourished Him.

St. Basil the Great

(329 – 379)

STS. BASIL AND GREGORY NAZIANZEN

Memorial, January 2

St. Basil and St. Gregory Nazianzen were born in Asia Minor, modern-day Turkey, around 329 or 330 AD. Both were born into Christian families. Their parents, some of their siblings, and their grandmothers all became saints!

Basil and Gregory were blessed with keen intellects and many opportunities for good educations. After being educated at home, Basil entered one of the schools at Caesarea where he met Gregory. They became good friends and excelled at their studies. When their coursework was completed, Basil went to Constantinople, and Gregory went to Alexandria and Palestine to study law. They were sad to leave each other but met again later in Athens, Greece, to finish their studies.

Both men were raised in strict Christian homes, but neither of them was baptized until after they finished their educations in Athens. Basil was attracted to the monastic life and studied with many holy monks. Returning home, he built a monastery on the Iris River and invited Gregory to join him. Gregory helped Basil with the monastery for two years but was called home to assist his elderly father, the bishop of Nazianzus, whose health was failing. Gregory was ordained to the priesthood at this time.

In 370 AD, Basil was made bishop of Caesarea to lead Catholics against the Arian influence of Emperor Valens. During this period in the Church, the heresy of Arianism was rampant. Basil appointed his friend, Gregory, to be the bishop of Sasima and restore order in the Church there. Gregory loved the life of the monk, not the life of controversy, and was deeply offended by Basil's decision to appoint him bishop without asking him first. A rupture in their friendship occurred which never completely healed. Gregory returned to Nazianzus to help his father, never governing the area of Sasima as bishop. When his father the bishop of Nazianzus died, Gregory moved to the mountains of Selucia, where he resumed living the life of a monk.

Basil continued the fight against the Arian emperors until his health failed in 379 AD. He lay on his deathbed, but upon seeing a number of men waiting to be ordained to the diaconate and the priesthood, he got up out of bed and ordained them. Then returning to bed, he died. Gregory was too sick to attend his friend's funeral, but later he wrote a public eulogy praising Basil's character and accomplishments.

In 381, Gregory presided over the Second Ecumenical Council at Ephesus. Later he was appointed patriarch of Constantinople. Troubles hounded Gregory in Constantinople. A group of Arians challenged his appointment. It was a difficult time for Gregory, who only wished to live the life of a monk. Moved by his eloquent preaching, scholars and the public flocked to hear him preach. Disturbed by the controversy, he decided to leave Constantinople. He preached an eloquent farewell speech and returned to the life of a monk, where he remained writing, praying, and gardening until his death in 389 AD. Gregory Nazianzen left a great treasury of writings. His poetry and prose are known for their theological depth and masterful style. Sts. Basil and Gregory Nazianzen are both Greek Fathers of the Catholic Church. Their writings and teachings are known for their doctrinal orthodoxy, antiquity, and approval by the Church. Each man was known for his personal sanctity.

ST. BASIL'S CRUMB CAKE
Level: Easy

St. Basil the Great, whose feast is celebrated on January 2 with St. Gregory Nazianzen in the General Roman Calendar, is honored by the Greeks with a cake called a *vasilopita*. It is a delicious coffee cake, and in the tradition of many festive foods, it contains a coin in it for good luck. Here is a quick recipe to enjoy with the family. According to Greek custom, the father of the family cuts the cake and saves the first piece for the Blessed Mother, then the next one for St. Basil. The rest of the family receives their piece according to age.

PREP: 15 minutes   **BAKE:** 20 - 25 minutes

INGREDIENTS   **EQUIPMENT**
1 egg   Measuring cups & spoons
¾ cup of milk   Large spoon or Wire whisk
2 cups Bisquick® baking mix   9-inch round pan
2 tablespoons of sugar   Mixing bowl
TOPPING
2 teaspoons cinnamon   Small bowl
¼ cup sugar   Baking spray
2 tablespoons Bisquick®   Coin
2 tablespoons unsalted butter
or margarine

DIRECTIONS: **YIELD:** 1 cake

1. Blend egg, milk, Bisquick®, and sugar.

2. Beat vigorously for 30 seconds with large spoon or wire whisk.

3. Spray 9-inch round pan with baking spray. Spread crumb cake mixture in pan.

4. For topping, put all ingredients in a small bowl; blend the ingredients with fork until crumbly.

5. Spread topping over crumb cake. Bake in preheated oven at 400 degrees Fahrenheit for 20 to 25 minutes. Test for doneness by inserting a toothpick or knife. If it comes out clean, the cake is ready. Remove from oven and cool.

6. I like to insert the coin just before we eat the cake, making sure no child is in danger of receiving it and swallowing it. You can insert a jelly bean or some other edible replacement as a safe substitute for the coin.

LESSON FOR SAINTS BASIL THE GREAT AND GREGORY NAZIANZEN

1. St. Basil and St. Gregory were bishops of the Catholic Church during the fourth century. They lived in what is now known as Turkey. They are Doctors of the Church. This is a special title given to saints whose writings and preaching are a benefit for all Catholics.

2. They are considered Greek Fathers of the Church because they wrote and taught in Greek.

3. St. Basil and St. Gregory were very good students and good friends. You can encourage your students to pray to them for the virtues of studiousness and genuine friendship.

4. They lived during difficult times in the Church. There were many false teachings about the faith that were circulating. St. Basil and Gregory wrote and preached the truths about Jesus Christ, that He is truly God and man. Both saints suffered for preaching these truths. Encourage the children to ask for the virtue of courage to proclaim the faith in season and out.

5. The central mystery of the Christmas season is that God sent His Son to become man, born of the Virgin Mary, to save us from our sins. Sts. Basil and Gregory taught this truth fearlessly with great clarity. We can honor them for their courage and celebrate their sainthood, reminding the children we are still in the Christmas season.

Share a treat and give out holy cards of these two great saints. You will find some beautiful holy cards online at www.catholicholycards.org

ST. ELIZABETH ANN SETON

Memorial, January 4

St. Elizabeth Ann Seton and St. John Neumann, the next saint we will discuss, are American saints known for their great contributions to Catholic school education among other things. Elizabeth Ann Seton was born in New York City, on August 28, 1774. She was from a prominent family who raised her in the Episcopalian faith. Her mother died when she was three, and her father, a doctor, then married Charlotte Barclay of the Roosevelt family. Elizabeth's stepmother often visited the poor and would take Elizabeth along with her. When she was nineteen, Elizabeth married William Seton, who was a wealthy merchant in the export/import business with his father and brother. The couple had five children, which kept Elizabeth very busy, but never too busy to assist those in need.

In the late 1790s a series of misfortunes befell the ships of the Seton mercantile business, and most of their wealth was lost. Subsequently, William Seton suffered poor health and in 1802, he

and Elizabeth traveled to Italy with their eldest daughter, Anna, hoping the climate would aid his recovery. The Setons were to stay as guests of the Filicchis, Italian business friends. Fearing the rumored yellow fever, the Italians insisted William be quarantined for a month before being allowed to join his friends. The family was released from quarantine on December 19, 1802, and allowed to go to Pisa, Italy. The Filicchis had arranged rooms for the family in Mrs. De Tot's house. On December 27 William Seton died, leaving Elizabeth a widow. The Filicchis invited Elizabeth and Anna to their home, where they lived for some months. During this time Elizabeth was introduced to the Catholic faith, particularly the Real Presence of Jesus in the Eucharist.

After her return to New York, Elizabeth pursued her study of the Catholic faith, sought and prayed for guidance and eventually entered the Catholic Church. Her family pleaded with her not to take such an extreme step and eventually disinherited her for becoming Catholic. Elizabeth as a result had very little money with which to raise her children. Some sympathetic friends suggested she teach. However this venture did not prove successful. A Sulpician priest from Baltimore, Fr. John Dubourg, suggested that she move there and start a Catholic girls' school. Her love of Jesus and the good priests who directed her gave her courage to leave New York and move to Baltimore. She arrived on the feast of Corpus Christi in1808. In Baltimore she supported her family by teaching young girls along with her own daughters. Her sons were educated by priests at St. Mary's College, Baltimore.

While in Baltimore Elizabeth took private vows under Archbishop John Carroll. Later in 1809, when a large donation was given for the purpose of educating poor children, she moved her school and those living with her to Emmitsburg, Maryland, where her work of education continued. Elizabeth, her daughters, and other women converts to the Catholic faith then formed a religious community whose rule was that of the Sisters of Charity founded by St. Vincent de Paul in France. Archbishop John Carroll approved the rule in 1812. Elizabeth Seton, against her wishes, was elected superior of the new religious congregation and was called Mother Seton.

Life in Emmitsburg was harsh and full of many privations. Death was a companion of this venture, but so were numerous vocations to the congregation. Many women joined this courageous group of religious who educated the young at Emmitsburg and who were also invited to serve in Philadelphia and New York before Mother Seton's death in 1821. There are many good biographies of Mother Seton which you will find in the resource section of this book. They provide more in-depth details of her conversion and perseverance in the life of faith. Mother Seton founded the first American congregation of religious women, the Sisters of Charity, and the first Catholic school. She was canonized by Pope Paul VI in 1975.

ST. JOHN NEUMANN

Memorial, January 5

Bishop John Neumann was born in Prachatitz, Bohemia, the present-day Czech Republic, on March 28, 1811. His father, Philip, was Bavarian and his mother, Agnes, Czech. They spoke German in the home. His parents had John baptized on the day he was born. His father was known for his generosity to the poor and his mother attended daily Mass, often bringing her children with her.

Neumann attended the University of Prague where he studied Theology. He applied to the local seminary in 1831. After completing his studies in Theology in 1835, he requested permission to be ordained to the priesthood. The local bishop denied his request saying there were too many priests in his diocese.

Neumann wrote to bishops throughout Europe seeking ordination. There were no positive responses. The United States had a great need for priests. Bishop John Dubois of the diocese of New York agreed to ordain him. Neumann studied English and then moved to New York where he was ordained to the priesthood by Bishop Dubois at Old St. Patrick's, New York City in 1836. His first assignments were in rural areas of New York State. He served there for a few years, but found the life very lonely. He requested permission to apply to a religious order called the Redemptorists. Permission was granted; he entered their candidacy program and was the first to take vows as a Redemptorist in the United States in 1842. As a Redemptorist priest he served in Baltimore, MD, and later in Pittsburgh, PA. In 1847 Fr. Neumann was appointed Superior of the Redemptorist Mission in the United States and the following year he became a naturalized citizen. In 1852 he was ordained as the fourth Bishop of Philadelphia, PA.

Bishop Neumann was a tireless worker for the Church and its people. In Philadelphia his zeal knew no bounds. During the eight years he served as bishop, he established the Catholic School System, enlarging it from two schools to one hundred. He brought religious sisters from Europe to serve in the schools and hospitals, organized and scheduled Forty Hours Eucharistic Devotion in all parishes, added a new parish every month, and preserved a black religious order from demise. His efforts were not without challenge. An anti-Catholic political group, the Know Nothings, sought to halt his progress by setting fires to schools and convents. Their efforts did not prevail, although they greatly discouraged Bishop Neumann.

Bishop Neumann was known for his frugality. He owned one pair of shoes. When given new vestments, he saved them for his newly ordained priests. As a priest he had learned many languages so he could serve the numerous ethnic groups flooding the United States. He knew eight. He learned Gaelic in order to hear the confessions of Irish immigrants in Philadelphia. The story

is told of one penitent who upon leaving the confessional remarked, "Glory be to God: an Irish bishop at last!" Bishop Neumann died of a heart attack on January 5, 1860, while running errands. He was only forty-eight years old and had given his all for Christ and the Catholic Church in the United States. He was canonized by Pope Paul VI in 1977. His feast day is January 5.

BREAD PUDDING
Level: Easy

Puddings were very common fare during the time of St. Elizabeth Ann Seton and St. John Neumann. They are not like the ones today that you whip up from a store-brought mix, light and creamy. Puddings were a heavier dessert, common to the everyday table and definitely tasty! Included here are two pudding recipes, modified a bit since the 1800s, but ones both saints would find familiar.

PREP: 20 minutes   **LET STAND:** 30 minutes   **BAKE:** 50 – 60 minutes

INGREDIENTS
12 – 16 slices of stale white bread
¾ cup raisins or other dried fruit
4 large eggs
3 cups whole milk
¾ cup of sugar
1 teaspoon vanilla
¾ teaspoon ground cinnamon
¼ teaspoon nutmeg
Pinch of salt, about 1/16 of a teaspoon!
Baking spray or butter

EQUIPMENT
2 quart baking dish
Large mixing bowl
Wire whisk
Measuring cups
Measuring spoons
Spatula
Knife or toothpick

DIRECTIONS:

1. Trim the crusts off the bread and cut into half-inch cubes. Spray baking dish with vegetable spray or grease with butter. Place the bread in the baking dish evenly. Add raisins or other dried fruit.

2. In a large mixing bowl combine eggs, milk, sugar, vanilla, cinnamon and nutmeg. Whisk them together completely.

3. Pour mixture over the bread and let stand for 30 minutes.

4. Preheat oven to 350 degrees Fahrenheit after assembling.

5. Bake between 50 – 60 minutes. Test for doneness by inserting a knife or toothpick in the center. If it comes out clean, it is done. Remove from oven and let cool. You may add whipped cream or ice cream as a topping if you like.

INDIAN PUDDING

Level: Moderate

Careful: Hot Milk

Corn was a vegetable found in the New World. Like St. Juan Diego in Mexico, the Indians in North America used corn, which they called *maize*, in many edible dishes. When the colonists came to the New World, they were introduced to corn by the Indians. It soon became a staple in their diets. St. John Neumann, when he served parishes in rural New York State, would undoubtedly have been offered Indian pudding by his parishioners, who incorporated cornmeal recipes into their everyday fare.

PREP: 20 minutes

BAKE: 70 minutes

INGREDIENTS

⅔ cup of cornmeal
4 cups of whole milk
⅓ cup sugar
¼ cup molasses
2 large eggs
2 tablespoons unsalted butter
1 teaspoon ground cinnamon
½ teaspoon ground ginger
⅛ teaspoon ground nutmeg
1 teaspoon vanilla
⅛ teaspoon salt
Baking spray or butter

EQUIPMENT

Large, heavy saucepan
2 quart baking dish
Measuring cups
Large spoon
Measuring spoons

DIRECTIONS: **YIELD:** 8 servings

1. Add ⅔ cup cornmeal into heavy saucepan; gradually stir in four cups of whole milk. While stirring constantly, bring to a boil over medium-high heat. Reduce the heat to low and simmer. Stir frequently until thick, about five minutes.

2. With a whisk add in sugar, molasses, eggs, butter cut into pieces, cinnamon, ginger, nutmeg, vanilla, and salt. Incorporate completely.

3. Pour pudding mixture into buttered or sprayed baking dish.

4. Preheat oven to 325 degrees Fahrenheit. Bake in oven about 70 minutes. Pudding will be ready when the center is firm but the edges are slightly jiggly!

LESSON FOR ST. ELIZABETH ANN SETON AND ST. JOHN NEUMANN

1. After reading the selections on St. Elizabeth Ann Seton and St. John Neumann ask the children what the two saints have in common. Some possible answers include the following: the period of time that they lived overlapped from 1811 – 1821. Both served God and the Catholic Church in the United States. St. Elizabeth was born in the U.S. and St. John Neumann became a naturalized citizen. They were involved in the education of youth, the formation of Catholic schools, and religious life. St. Elizabeth Ann Seton founded the first community of religious women in Maryland, while St. John Neumann was the first Redemptorist in the U.S.

2. Let the children explore and discuss the many talents and virtues each saint modeled. St. Elizabeth Seton received a good education because her family had financial means. She was blessed with the good examples of her father who was a doctor and served the sick and her stepmother whose charity reached out to the poor. These good examples taught Elizabeth to show concern for those in need. Another virtue that she excelled in was courage. When her husband's business and then his health failed, they moved to Italy. After William Seton's death, Elizabeth became Catholic. As a result of her conversion, her wealthy relatives withdrew the money she needed to support her fatherless children. However, Elizabeth did not give up. She was courageous. She moved to another state; she started the first Catholic school and formed a religious community of women to serve the Church. Although born into wealth and comfort she was not attached to them. Love of God and His Will were her guides.

3. St. John Neumann studied to become a priest but was turned down by his own bishop. He did not give up. He wrote to bishops until he received an invitation to be ordained in a foreign country. He had to learn a new language but he did not let that stop him. He became very lonely in one rural location he was assigned to as a priest and learned that, for most people, living in community makes us happy. He asked his bishop to let him live in community. It takes humility to admit we need to change sometimes. St. John Neumann had humility.

4. There are many lessons we can learn from the lives of St. Elizabeth Ann Seton and St. John Neumann. Choose the lessons that fit with your children. Then honor these wonderful role models by asking for their help, watching a movie about them, baking a treat and sharing information about their lives with your family and friends.

God and man, your songs of praise
To the flute and drum now raise!
God and man, your song now praise
To the flute and drum now raise!
Tu-re-lu-re-lu, Pata-pata pan,
To the savior sing Noel.

from the French Christmas carol *Pat-a-pan*
by Bernard de La Monnoye
(June 15, 1641 – October 15, 1728)

ST. ANDRÉ BESSETTE

Optional Memorial, January 6

January 7 in Canada

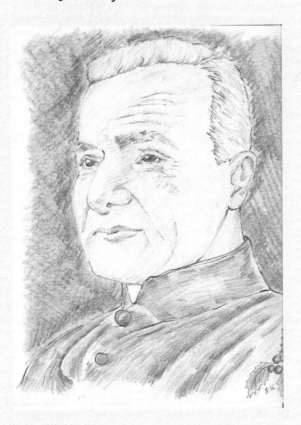

Born on August 9, 1845, St. André was the eighth of twelve children. His parents, Isaac and Clothilde, were a pious couple who named their little son Alfred. A sickly infant, Alfred was conditionally baptized on the day he was born.

His family was poor; however, despite their poverty they were quite happy. They lived about twenty-five miles southeast of Montreal, Canada, in a one-room cabin, twenty feet by seventeen feet. Alfred's father died when he was only nine years old, leaving his mother with little means of supporting the family.

Due to his delicate health, Alfred did not go to school regularly, and as a result he did not learn to read or write until his mid-twenties. His poor health caused his mother to favor him with extra attention and a place right beside her during the evening rosary. Her love of the faith and instruction fostered a deep love of the faith in him. He loved to pray and talk to St. Joseph in

his spare time. How sad it was for Alfred when at age twelve his mother died. Shortly after that he went to live with his Uncle Timothy's family.

It was soon decided that Alfred should learn a trade. This was the beginning of a number of trades that he would attempt to learn, none with great success. His delicate health and lack of stamina deterred him from mastering any of them. After working first in Canada and then for a few years in the United States, he returned to Canada where his pastor, Rev. André Provencal, offered him part-time employment. In his spare time, he spent many hours in church praying and talking to St. Joseph.

In 1870 at the recommendation of Rev. Provencal, Alfred applied to the novitiate of the Congregation of Holy Cross as a lay brother. The parish priest is quoted as telling the order's superior, "I am sending you a saint." After one year with the order, they declined to allow Alfred to take vows because of health reasons. During the same period, the Archbishop of Montreal visited the Holy Cross Congregation. Seeing his chance, Alfred stole into the room when the archbishop was alone. Looking downcast, the archbishop asked him what the trouble was. Alfred told him his story, imploring the archbishop to allow him to remain. With a brief response he assured Alfred that he would be allowed to join the order. On February 2, 1874, St. André's baptismal name of Alfred was forever changed to André. Final vows were pronounced and he became a lay brother of the Congregation of Holy Cross, assigned as a porter to the Notre Dame College.

For forty years Br. André was a porter at the Notre Dame College, a school for boys ages seven to twelve. It was there that he answered the door, welcomed guests, woke up boarders, and delivered mail. His health continued to bother him. Often his only nourishment was flour dropped in boiling water and a watered-down milk drink. However, his prayer life and devotion to St. Joseph thrived. As his devotion deepened, he was inspired to recommend it to others who came to his porter's door seeking help.

Two characteristics of Br. André stand out: his love of St. Joseph and his love of those in need. Over his years as a porter, his reputation for assisting the needy grew. The sick would come to him; he would rub their ailments with oil, give them a medal of St. Joseph, and pray to St. Joseph with them. Many miraculous healings took place. Br. André always said it was St. Joseph who was interceding with God for the healing. It was St. Joseph who Br. André wanted honored and thanked.

In 1904 Br. André asked permission to build a chapel to St. Joseph on the mountain near Notre Dame College. The Archbishop of Montreal gave permission but with the stipulation that he raise the necessary money; he was not allowed to borrow money. Since Br. André only had a few hundred dollars to his name, the chapel to St. Joseph started out small, as a shelter where Mass could be said and pilgrims could come to honor St. Joseph. For many years it remained very modest, slowly changing from a shelter to a small stone chapel. In 1924 Br. André received permission to begin building a large basilica named St. Joseph's Oratory on the side of the mountain near the stone chapel. The devotion of the pilgrims to St. Joseph and Br. André, the miraculous healings of body and soul, and the donations given made the building of a large basilica possible.

The building of St. Joseph's Oratory, however, did not proceed unimpeded. It suffered from a lack of funds. In 1936 with construction halted for a number of years, the Council of the Oratory considered the future of the project. The basilica was without a roof, a dome. Br. André listened as various solutions were discussed. Finally he spoke, "We all want to cover the basilica as soon as possible. Let us put a statue of St. Joseph within its unfinished walls. He will soon find a roof for himself!" Soon a plan was devised. Funds were raised and the project was resumed.

At this point, Br. André's health was failing. No longer the porter at Notre Dame College, he continued encouraging devotion to St. Joseph and ministering to the sick and needy. He did not live to see his greatest dream realized—the Oratory of St. Joseph completed. He died on January 6, 1937, at ninety-one years of age. The Oratory was finally finished in 1967, a testament to Br. André's love and devotion to St. Joseph, the foster father of Our Lord and the spouse of the Blessed Mother. Br. André was canonized on October 17, 2010, by Pope Benedict XVI and is now known as St. André of Montreal.

MAPLE SUGAR CANDY

Level: Moderate

Caveat: Boiling liquids

St. André grew up in French Canada. The area is well-known for its maple syrup and its many recipes made from maple syrup. Here is a simple and delicious recipe using this tasty liquid. Be sure that an adult supervises the making of the candy since it involves very high temperatures.

PREP: 1 minute

COOK: 10 minutes

INGREDIENTS
2 cups of maple syrup
(not artificial syrup)

EQUIPMENT
One heavy-bottom, medium- sized saucepan
Measuring cups
Large spoon
Candy thermometer
Candy molds, leaf shape if
possible, small size

DIRECTIONS:

YIELD: 16 pieces

1. Pour 2 cups of real maple syrup into a medium-sized, heavy-bottom saucepan.

2. Bring maple syrup to a boil over medium-high heat. Stir the liquid occasionally until it reaches 240 degrees Fahrenheit.

3. Remove from heat and let cool to 200 degrees, checking your candy thermometer.

4. At 200 degrees stir continually until the liquid has a sugary consistency but has not hardened.

5. Spoon into molds and let harden.

6. When candy has cooled, unmold and enjoy it. Yum.

MAPLE SYRUP MUFFINS
Level: Easy

Here is a treat for a cold winter's breakfast. These muffins are fun and easy to make. You can bake them the night before and just warm them up in the morning if you are in a hurry.

PREP: 15 minutes   **BAKE:** 25 minutes

INGREDIENTS

1 egg
¼ cup vegetable oil
½ cup pure maple syrup
½ cup of milk
¼ cup of sugar
2 cups all-purpose flour
3 teaspoons baking powder
½ teaspoon baking soda
½ teaspoon salt
1 cup finely chopped
nuts (optional)

EQUIPMENT

Muffin tin (12)
Cupcake liners or Cooking
spray
2 small mixing bowls
Electric mixer
Measuring cups
Measuring spoons
Large spoon
Ice cream scoop (optional)

DIRECTIONS: **YIELD:** 12 muffins

1. Lightly spray or oil muffin tin or line with cupcake liners. Preheat oven to 375 degrees Fahrenheit.

2. Beat egg, oil, maple syrup and milk together in one bowl.

3. Mix dry ingredients in another bowl, then add dry ingredients to wet ingredients stirring just until blended. Do not overbeat.

4. Fill muffin cups each ⅔ full.

5. Bake for 20 - 25 minutes or until lightly browned.

6. Remove from oven and let cool. Serve with pure maple butter, jelly, or your favorite spread.

LESSON FOR THE FEAST OF ST. ANDRÉ BESSETTE

St. André's feast day is the last saint celebration in this book. His great devotion to St. Joseph reminds us of how St. Joseph cooperated with God's plan to send His Son to the human family and restore grace to us. Let us take advantage of the last graces unique to the Christmas season by honoring St. André and St. Joseph together.

1. Summarize the details of the life of St. André or read a short story that would appeal to the ages of your children. You might want to focus on his poor health. Ask the children how his poor health helped him to draw closer to Our Lord and St. Joseph in prayer. St. André developed the habits of compassion and prayer in his life through and because of his experience of poor health. Encourage the children to describe what it means to be compassionate and prayerful.

2. St. André did not learn to read or write until he was in his twenties. Some children struggle with learning to read or write or both! They can turn to St. André and ask him to give them the strength to persevere in what is a difficult task for them. Pray to St. André for the virtue of fortitude.

3. St. André had a great devotion to St. Joseph, who is the foster father of Jesus, the husband of Mary, and the patron of the universal Church. I believe it would please Jesus very much to end *Celebrating Advent and Christmas with Children* by honoring St. André and St. Joseph together and directing our thanks to those two saints who have helped and continue to help both children and adults with their physical and spiritual needs.

4. Enjoy some of the maple candies to honor St. André and St. Joseph. If you don't have time to make the candies, you can buy them in many stores or order them online. There are many recipes which use maple syrup. You might choose to make a cake or pudding or try the muffin recipe included in this book. Whatever you do, celebrate this wonderful saint and his devotion to St. Joseph. If you have prayer cards, share them with all in your party.

Now when Jesus was born in Bethlehem of Judea in the days of Herod the king, behold, Wise Men from the East came to Jerusalem, saying, "Where is he who has been born king of the Jews? For we have seen his star in the East, and have come to worship him." . . . And behold, the star which they had seen in the East went before them, till it came to rest over the place where the child was. When they saw the star, they rejoiced exceedingly with great joy; and going into the house they saw the child with Mary his mother, and they fell down and worshipped him. Then, opening their treasures they offered him gifts, gold and frankincense and myrrh. (Matthew 2:1-2, 9-11)

EPIPHANY

Solemnity, January 6

(Observed on the Sunday after the Octave of Christmas)

In some Catholic countries, such as Spain, Epiphany has traditionally been the day of gift-giving. Early in the Church's history, it was observed by some as the day to celebrate Christ's birth. Since the fourth century the Church has selected December 25 as the day of celebration.

The word epiphany means "manifestation." Its roots are Greek, and in the ancient Greco-Roman world an *epiphaneia* indicated an official state visit by a king to the subjects in his kingdom. The first *epiphaneia* to the Gentiles occurred when the Magi visited Jesus in the stable in Bethlehem. It was there that God revealed his Son to those who were not Jews. This feast is a solemn one in the Church and is celebrated on the Sunday after the Solemnity of Mary, the Mother of God.

There are many Catholic culinary and cultural traditions observed on Epiphany by the Spanish and French and among those they colonized. The English, Portuguese, Danes and Italians have their store of traditions, too. The most well-known is the King's Cake or Twelfth Night Cake, which is the crowning touch at a party that symbolizes the close of the Christmas culinary season.

Although the recipes for King's Cake vary from country to country, two features are common to all. The cake is special; it is rich to indicate a great feast. And it always contains one bean, coin, or small trinket, the recipient of which is designated to host the next party. Some customs demand the party be given on February 2, Candlemas Day. Others require a party on Mardi Gras, featuring another King's Cake with a hidden token to insure a long line of future parties! Since the week following Epiphany is still in the Christmas season, it is quite fitting to celebrate the feast at home, school, or CCD class. Decorating the King's Cake guarantees lots of fun for those participating and a beautiful way to bring to a close our Christmas celebrations.

KING'S CAKE
Or King's Cupcakes
Level: Easy

PREP: 10 minutes   **BAKE:** 45 to 50 minutes   **DECORATE:** 10 minutes
25 minutes for cupcakes

INGREDIENTS	EQUIPMENT
Cake mix or store-bought cake	Large mixing bowl
Eggs	Measuring cups
Vegetable oil	Large spoon
Water	Electric mixer
Baking spray	Bundt pan or 2 cupcake
Flour	pans
Prepared frosting	Cupcake liners
Jelly beans, gum drops,	Doily
Hershey's® Kisses, or other candy	Gold foil play crowns
	Coin, Trinket, or Bean

DIRECTIONS:

YIELD: 1 bundt cake
24 cupcakes

1. Preheat oven to 350 degrees Fahrenheit and prepare as directed on box.

2. Spray the Bundt pan with baking spray and lightly flour. Pour cake batter into pan.

3. Drop a gumdrop in the batter as a substitute for the coin. Bake according to directions. If you choose to make cupcakes, line the cupcake pan with cupcake liners, add batter, then place gumdrop in one of the cupcakes.

4. Remove from oven and cool. With a knife, loosen cake and gently turn it onto plate lined with a doily. (Remove cupcakes from pan.)

5. Frost the cake generously. Remember this is a King's Cake! Frost inside of Bundt hole.

6. Decorate with colored gum drops or other candy that makes the cake look like a crown full of jewels. You may add a gold foil crown on the top of the Bundt cake as a finishing touch. (Decorate cupcakes to look like mini-crowns; they look terrific and display well.)

7. Display the cake in a prominent place. If you have crowns for everyone, now is the time to put them on and sing "We Three Kings!"

BALTHAZARS

Level: Moderate

* Nuts

This is a chocolate candy named after the Ethiopian Balthazar, one of the Magi who jour-neyed to Bethlehem to pay homage to the newborn King. Balthazar's gift to the baby Jesus was myrrh, a spice used for burial. The recipe is quite simple* and takes little time; however, it must be chilled for 48 hours before eating.

PREP: 20 minutes   **CHILL:** 30 minutes   **CHILL:** 2 days

INGREDIENTS	**EQUIPMENT**
8 ounces (squares) semisweet chocolate	Grater
1 pound shelled whole walnuts	Chopper
½ cup plus 1 tablespoon confectioners' sugar	Measuring cups
1 ½ tablespoon rum or orange juice	Medium-sized mixing bowl
1 tablespoon grated orange rind	Wax paper
1 or 2 egg whites, as needed	

DIRECTIONS: **YIELD:** 6 dozen slices

1. Finely grate chocolate and half of the walnuts.

2. Remaining walnuts should be more coarsely chopped or grated.

3. Mix chocolate and finely grated walnuts. Add sugar, orange juice, and orange rind.

4. Stir in enough egg white to moisten mixture. Then pack firmly. If mixture is too wet, add more sugar or nuts.

5. Chill for 30 minutes.

6. Divide mixture into three balls.

7. Form the three balls into logs about 1 inch around and eight to ten inches long. Roll the logs in the coarsely chopped walnuts, wrap in waxed paper and chill for at least 2 days.

8. Cut in slices just before serving.

*The skill level for grating is more advanced than an easy recipe would indicate.
Reprinted with permission from *Visions of Sugarplums* by Mimi Sheraton.

STAINED GLASS STAR COOKIES
Level: Easy

What did the wise men say? "We have seen His star." Here are some stars you can enjoy making with your bakers as we prepare to celebrate the Solemnity of the Epiphany.

PREP: 25 minutes   **BAKE:** as directed on package

INGREDIENTS   **EQUIPMENT**
Refrigerated sugar cookie dough   Floured surface
Life Savers candy, multi-colored Rolling pin
Baking spray   Star cookie cutters
Baking sheets   Wax paper

DIRECTIONS: **YIELD:** 12 to 24 cookies

1. Follow directions for cookie dough on package. Check oven temperature.

2. Roll out dough and cut in shape of stars.

3. Place one cookie star on baking sheet. Take the second cookie star and cut out a smaller star from inside of it. Set small star aside.

4. Crush life savers between two pieces of wax paper.

5. Place second star on top of the first star and add a small amount of crushed life savers to the cut-out center area.

6. Be sure all parts of the cookie are attached to each other by gently pressing together.

7. Repeat until all stars are used. Bake according to the directions.

8. Bake smaller cut-out stars separately, as they will bake in a shorter period of time.

LESSON FOR EPIPHANY

1. Read the Gospel account of the Visit of the Magi (see Matthew 2: 1–11) to your children.

2. Discuss with them what a great journey the Magi had undertaken to find the King of the Jews. Explain that the Magi were not Jews themselves. Recall the story of God's promise to Abraham, the patriarch of the Hebrews, that the Savior would be sent through his family line. On Epiphany we celebrate God's revealing his divine Son, Jesus, to the three kings. The feast of the Epiphany makes manifest the baby Jesus as the divine King who is sent as the Savior of all people, the Jews and the Gentiles. The Magi brought gifts of gold, frankincense and myrrh. For older children you might discuss the significance of the gifts they brought for Jesus: gold for His kingship, frankincense for His priesthood, and myrrh for His burial.

3. Celebrate this great feast by decorating a home-made or store-bought Bundt cake. See the King's Cake recipe for directions. Cupcakes are always fun, and you might also try the Balthazars, or Stained Glass Star Cookies. Inexpensive gold crowns can be purchased from most party or dollar stores for the children to wear. Making the crowns is fun, too! You can trace crown patterns on paper or card stock and have the children color and cut them out. A couple of staples or tape will hold them in place for your party. End the class with the song "We Three Kings."

RESOURCES

COLORS FOR THE LITURGICAL SEASONS

GREEN   ORDINARY TIME

VIOLET   ADVENT, LENT, MASS FOR LIFE (FUNERAL OPTIONAL)

RED   MARTYRS, PALM SUNDAY, PENTECOST,
CONFIRMATION, GOOD FRIDAY, MASS OF THE HOLY SPIRIT

WHITE   EASTER, CHRISTMAS, FEASTS, MEMORIALS
(FUNERAL OPTIONAL)

ROSE   THIRD SUNDAY OF ADVENT AND FOURTH SUNDAY OF LENT
(OPTIONAL)

BLACK   ALL SOULS (FUNERAL OPTIONAL)

LITURGICAL SYMBOLS FOR ADVENT AND CHRISTMAS

SEASON: CHRISTMAS

THE MANGER

The most familiar symbol of Christ's nativity. It should be designed simply, representing the humble setting of the birth celebration of God. The symbol to the right has added the sacred monogram for Jesus (the first three letters from the Greek word for Jesus, IHCOYC) and the crown symbolizing Jesus the King of Kings.

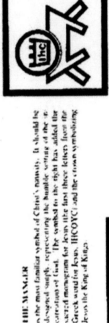

THE BURNING BUSH

An Old Testament symbol adopted by the Christian Church and applied to the theme of Christ's incarnation. God spoke to Moses from a burning bush (Ex. 3). Medieval writers paralleled God's coming to man in a burning bush with God's coming to man as an infant. In this way the burning bush became a symbol for the nativity of Jesus.

THE HOLLY WREATH

has become a widely used symbol during the Christmas season. Holly has a spiny-edged leaf and bright red berries. The foliage and berries in the form of a wreath symbolize the crown of thorns and the drops of blood, reminding us that during the celebration of the incarnation we must not forget the purpose of Christ's coming.

THE HERALDIC ANGEL

with hands raised in benediction is a symbol of the nativity. We associate such figures with the angelic message to the shepherds. The word "angel" comes from the Greek word meaning "messenger".

SEASON: ADVENT

Advent is the beginning season of the Christian Church year. There are four Sundays in Advent. These four weeks provide a period of preparation for the coming of Christ, culminating in the celebration of the incarnation at Christmas. The Christian Church should emphasize the symbols of Advent because much of the true meaning and preparation is lost amidst numerous non-Christian decorations and images.

SUN AND CHI RHO

One of the most beautiful descriptions of the Messiah is in the last chapter of the Old Testament. Christ is referred to as "The Sun of Righteousness" (Malachi 4:2). The sun is the source of light. In Christian thought Jesus was referred to as the light. "In Him was life, and the life was the light of men" (John 1:4). The symbol to the left combines the sun with the Chi Rho, a familiar symbol for Christ (see above).

MESSIANIC ROSE

The rose has various meanings in Christian symbolism. The Messianic Rose is described in the thirty fifth chapter of Isaiah where the prophet writes that the desert shall rise as a rose at the coming of the glory of God. Thus advent symbolizes the coming of God in Jesus Christ.

THE BRANCH

The Branch is another Messianic or prophetic symbol. Zechariah wrote: "Behold, I will bring my Servant, the Branch" (3:8). Jeremiah wrote: "Behold, the days are coming, says the Lord, when I will raise up for David a righteous Branch" (23:5). The branch is also associated with the first Sunday in Advent because the Gospel lesson describes the spreading of branches before Christ as he entered the city of Jerusalem.

THE LAMB OF GOD

When John the Baptist saw Jesus he said, "Behold the Lamb of God" (in Latin, Ecce Agnus Dei) who takes away the sin of the world" (John 1:29). This is a meaningful message during the Advent season when all men are called to witness the coming of Jesus, the Christ. The lamb has the three-rayed nimbus to designate a member of the Trinity.

BOOKS AND DVDS FOR CHILDREN

Liturgical Year, Advent Wreath, Advent Calendar, and Holly Wreath

Print Media:

Advent-Christmas Book, by Joan Marie Arbogast. Pauline Books & Media, Boston, MA.

Advent, Christmas, and Epiphany in the Domestic Church, by Catherine and Peter Fournier. Ignatius Press, San Francisco, CA.

Family Celebrations: Advent and Christmas, by Jane Beaton, Wanda Doppler, Greg Gallagher, and Betty Hardy. The Liturgical Press, Collegeville, MN.

Feast Days & Holy Days: Color-by-Number Book, by Mary Elizabeth Tebo, FSP, Kathryn James Hermes, FSP, and Virginia Helen Richards, FSP. (English and Spanish editions). Pauline Books & Media, Boston, MA.

Free Catholic Coloring Pages, assembled by Julie Luckey. St. John the Baptist Catholic Church, Front Royal, VA., http://www.sjtb.org/

A Handbook of Catholic Sacramentals, by Ann Ball. Our Sunday Visitor, Huntington, IN.

Our Year with God: A Child's Introduction to Catholic Holy Days and the Liturgical Year, by Natalie Kadela. Pauline Books & Media, Boston, MA, or Amazon.com.

Prayers around the Crib, by Juliette Levivier. Magnificat, Ignatius Press, San Francisco, CA.

The Sacramentals of the Church, by Fr. Lawrence G. Lovasik, SVD. Catholic Book Publishing Co., NY.

Signs & Symbols in Christian Art, by George Ferguson. Oxford University Press, London, Oxford, NY.

Symbols of Church Seasons & Days, by John Bradner. Morehouse Publishing, Harrisburg, PA.

A Wreath of Christmas Legends, by Phyllis McGinley, The MacMillan Co., New York, available on amazon.com

Audiovisual Materials:

Advent Calendar, DVD, 100 minutes. Twenty-five mini-documentaries explaining the symbolism of the wreath, candy cane, Handel's *Messiah,* and more.www.videoswithvalues.org

Advent Calendar II, DVD, 155 minutes. Explains Christmas carols and hymns. www.videoswithvalues.org

Advent: Celebrating the Season, video, 12 minutes, grades 3 – 8. Oblate Media and Communication, Florissant, MO. www.videoswithvalues.org

St. Nicholas

Print Media:

How St. Nicholas Became Santa Claus: The True Story (Project Book), by Deacon Bernie Marquis and Theresa Myers. Pauline Books & Media, Boston, MA.

The Legend of Saint Nicholas, by Margaret K. Demi. McElderry Books, Simon & Schuster Children's Publishing Division, New York, N.Y.

Loyola Kids Book of Saints, by Amy Welborn. Loyola Press, Chicago, IL, 2001.

The Miracle of St. Nicholas, by Gloria Whelan. Ignatius Press, San Francisco, CA, 2001.

The True Saint Nicholas: Why He Matters to Christmas, by William J. Bennet. Howard Books, A Division of Simon and Schuster, Inc., New York, NY.

The True Story of Santa Claus, by Paul Prokop. Pauline Books & Media, Boston, MA.

Audiovisual Materials:

Advent with St. Nicholas: Customs from around the World, by Alison Berger, video, 20 minutes, ages: 7 – 11. www.videoswithvalues.org

Nicholas, Stephen, Anne and Joachim, Saints for Kids Vol. II, video with discussion and activity guide. Script adapted by Marie Paul Curley, FSP. Pauline Books & Media, Boston, MA.

Nicholas: The Boy Who Became Santa, video/DVD, 30 minutes, Ignatius Press, San Francisco, CA.

Saints' Gallery Vol. III: Saints for All Seasons (Mary, St. Valentine, St. Patrick, St. Nicholas and others), video, 40 minutes. Oblate Media and Communication, Florissant, MO.

Organizations:
St. Nicholas Center: Discovering the Truth about Santa Claus. An organization devoted to the education of the faithful and the wider public about the true St. Nicholas. You will find extensive book recommendations for children, recipes, cookies cutters, plays, skits, crafts, and much more. www.stnicholascenter.org

The Immaculate Conception

Print Media:
I Meet Mary, by Joseph Codina and Roser Ruis. Pauline Books & Media, Boston, MA.

Immaculate Conception, St. Joseph Picture Books, Catholic Book Publishing Co., Totowa, NJ.

Marian Devotion in the Catholic Church, by Peter and Catherine Fournier. Ignatius Press, San Francisco, CA.

Mary Most Holy (**coloring book**), by Katherine Sotik. Ignatius Press, San Francisco, CA.

Mary My Mother, by Fr. Lawrence G. Lovasik, SVD. St. Joseph Picture Books, Catholic Book Publishing Co., Totowa, NJ.

Mary: The Mother of Jesus, by Tomie de Paola. Holiday Publishing House, New York, NY., available amazon.com

My First Book about Mary, by Christine V. Orfeo, FSP, illus. by Julia Darrenkamp, FSP. Pauline Books & Media, Boston, MA.

My First Prayers with Mary, by Maïte Roche. Magnificat, Ignatius Press, San Francisco, CA.

My First Pictures of Mary, by Maïte Roche. Magnificat, Ignatius Press, San Francisco, CA.

Juan Diego/Our Lady of Guadalupe

Print Media:
Juan Diego: Mary's Humble Messenger, by Barbara Yoffie. Liguori Publications, Liguori, MO.

Loyola Kids Book of Saints, by Amy Welborn. Loyola Press, Chicago, IL, 2001.

Our Lady of Guadalupe, by Jose Luis Guerrero. Liguori Publications, Liguori, MO.

Our Lady of Guadalupe, by Tomie de Paola. Holiday Publishing House, New York, NY., available amazon.com.

Our Lady of Guadalupe, St. Joseph Picture Books. Catholic Book Publishing Co., Totowa, NJ.

Our Lady of Guadalupe for Children / Nuestra Senora de Guadalupe para Ninos, by Lupita Vital, Liguori Publications, Liguori, MO.

Praise Him With Your Very Life: A Collection of Plays, by Mother Mary Francis, PCC. One short play in a book of six plays, "Our Lady of Guadalupe," cast of twelve, 4th grade and up. Catholic Heritage Curricula, email: chc@chcweb.com www.Catholicheritagecurricula.com.

St. Juan Diego and Our Lady of Guadalupe, by Josephine Nobisso. Pauline Books & Media, Boston, MA.

Audiovisual Materials:
Juan Diego: Messenger of Guadalupe, DVD, 30 minutes, Ignatius Press, San Francisco, CA.

Once On a Barren Hill: The Story of Our Lady of Guadalupe, video, 27 minutes. Classic story of Our Lady Guadalupe, available amazon.com.

Our Lady of Guadalupe, video, 70 minutes. Ignatius Press, San Francisco, CA.

St. Lucy

Print Media:
Celebrating Christmas, by Fr. Jude Winkler, OFM. Conv. St. Joseph Picture Books, Catholic Book Publishing Co., Totowa, NJ. St. Lucy is featured on pages 18 &19.

Lucia Child of Light: The History and Traditions of Sweden's Lucia Celebration, by Florence Ekstrand. Skandisk, Inc. ,Bloomington, MN. www.skandisk.com.

Lucia Saint of Light, by Katherine Bolger Hyde. Conciliar Press, Ben Lomond, CA, 2008.

Saints of Christmas Activity Book, by Katherine Borgatti. Ligouri Publications, Ligouri, MO, 2013.

Swedish Coloring and Activity Book, St. Lucia Crown with electric candles or soft Lucia Crown, may be ordered online from Scandinavian Touch. These items are seasonal from September through December. Contact by phone: 215-813-1315   http://scandinaviantouch.com.

Las Posadas

Print Media:
Celebrating Christmas, by Fr. Jude Winkler, OFM. Conv. St. Joseph Picture Books, Catholic Book Publishing, Co., Totowa, NJ. *Las Posadas* is described on pages 24 &25.

Las Posadas: A Bilingual Celebration for Children, by Kathryn J. Hermes, FSP, and Mary Monge. Pauline Books and Media, Boston, MA.

Las Posadas: A Hispanic Christmas Celebration, by Diane Hoyt-Goldsmith. Holiday House Publishing, New York, NY.

Nine Days to Christmas: A Story of Mexico by Marie Hall Ets & Aurora Labastida. The Viking Press, New York, NY.

The Night of Las Posadas, by Tomie de Paola. Holiday House Publishing, New York, NY., available amazon.com

Paradise Tree   (See "Baking Resources" for more information)
Adam and Eve Cookie Molds with the Paradise Tree. House on the Hill, email info@houseonthehill.net or go to www.houseonthehill.net.

Crèches

Print Media:
Brother Francis and the Christmas Surprise, by Mildred Corell Luckhardt, Paulist Press, Ramsey, NJ. Out of print, available on amazon.com

Celebrating Christmas by Fr. Jude Winkler, OFM. Conv. St. Joseph Picture Books, Catholic Book Publishing, Co., Totowa, NJ. The Christmas crib is described on pages 10-11.

The Christmas Crèche: Treasure of Faith, Art, & Theater, by Matthew Powell, OP. Crèche scenes from around the world. Pauline Books & Media, Boston, MA.

Praise Him With Your Very Life: A Collection of Plays by Mother Mary Francis, PCC. One short play in a book of six plays, "Christmas at Greccio: A Christmas Play in One Act." Catholic Heritage Curricula, email: chc@chcweb.com or www.Catholicheritagecurricula.com.

Christmas: The Birth of Jesus

Print Media:
The Birthday of Jesus, by Nadia Bonaido. Pauline Books & Media, Boston, MA.

Book of Christmas Carols, by Tomie de Paola. Holiday House Publishing, New York, NY.

Celebrating Christmas, by Fr. Jude Winkler, OFM. Conv., St. Joseph Picture Books, Catholic Book Publishing, Co., Totowa, NJ. Christmas Day is described on pages 2 & 3, and the true meaning of Christmas on 30 & 31.

Jesus in the Manger, by Maïte Roche. Magnificat, Ignatius Press, San Francisco, CA.

My First Pictures of Christmas, by Maïte Roche. Magnificat, Ignatius Press, San Francisco, CA.

My First Prayers for Christmas, by Maïte Roche. Magnificat, Ignatius Press, San Francisco, CA.

The Donkey's Dream, by Barbara Helen Berger. Philomel, an imprint of Penguin Books, New York, NY.

The First Christmas Story (Coloring Book). Pauline Books & Media, Boston, MA.

The Friendly Beasts, by Tomie de Paola. Holiday House Publishing, New York, NY.

The Man Born to Be King, by Dorothy L. Sayers. Ignatius Press, San Francisco, CA. Dramas with scripts to be read or acted out, ages 7 to adult.

The Story of Baby Jesus, by M. Luzi. Pauline Books & Media, Boston, MA.

When Jesus Was Born: The Story of the Very First Christmas, by Magdalena Kim, FSP. Pauline Books & Media, Boston, MA.

Audiovisual Materials:

We Celebrate the Birth of Jesus, DVD/CD. Adoremus Books, Omaha, NE.

WEE Sing for Christmas, by Pamela Conn Beall and Susan Hagen Nipp.

St. Elizabeth Ann Seton

Print Media:

Elizabeth Ann Seton: Mother for Many, by Barbara Yoffie. Liguori Publications, Liguori, MO.

Kat Finds a Friend: A St. Elizabeth Ann Seton Story, by Joan Stromberg. Ecce Homo Press, an imprint of Behold Publications, Buckner, KY. www.beholdpublications.com.

Loyola Kids Book of Saints, by Amy Welborn. Loyola Press, Chicago, IL, 2001.

Mother Seton and the Sister of Charity (Vision Books) by Alma Power-Waters (Jul 7, 2000).

Saint Elizabeth Ann Seton – Daughter of America, by Jeanne Marie Grunwell. Pauline Books & Media, Boston, MA.

Saint Elizabeth Ann Seton, by Lawrence G. Lovasik, SVD, Catholic Book Publishing, Totowa, NJ.

Audiovisual Materials:

A Time for Miracles, DVD, starring Kate Mulgrew, et al. (Jun 1, 1980) www.amazon.com

Saint Elizabeth Ann Seton, DVD, by Bob and Penny Lord, 2010, www.bobandpennylord.com

St. John Neumann

Print Media:

Little Book of Saints, Volume 4 (St. John Neumann and more) by Susan Helen Wallace, FSP. Pauline Book & Media, Boston, MA.

Loyola Kids Book of Saints, by Amy Welborn. Loyola Press, Chicago, IL, 2001.

St. John Neumann: Do Whatever He Tells You, by Brenda and George Nippert. Nippert & Company Art Works, Carlisle, PA. www.catholicartworks.com.

Thomas Finds a Treasure: A St. John Neumann Story, by Joan Stromberg. Behold Publications, Buckner, KY.

Audiovisual Materials:
St. John Neumann: Fourth Bishop of Philadelphia, DVD hosted by Bob and Penny Lord, http://www.bobandpennylord.com

St. André Bessette

Print Media:
André Bessette: A Heart of Strength, by Barbara Yoffie. Liguori Publications, Liguori, MO.

Little Book of Saints, Volume 4 (St. André Bessette and more) by Susan Helen Wallace, FSP. Pauline Book & Media, Boston, MA.

Saint André Bessette: Miracles in Montreal, by Patricia Edward Jablonski, FSP. Pauline Books & Media, Boston, MA.

Audiovisual Materials:
God's Doorkeeper: St. André of Montreal. Available on Amazon.com

Epiphany

Print Media:
Celebrating Christmas, by Fr. Jude Winkler, OFM. Conv. St. Joseph Picture Books, Catholic Book Publishing, Co., Totowa, NJ. Epiphany and the Befania tradition from Italy are described on pages 22 & 23.

The Story of the Other Wise Man, by Henry van Dyke. Paraclete Press, Brewster, MA.

The Story of the Three Wise Kings, by Tomie de Paola. Holiday House Publishing, New York, NY.

Three Kings and a Star, by Fred Crump, Jr. Adoremus Books, Omaha, NE.

BLOGS AND WEBSITES

The following blogs and websites offer extensive resources for following the seasons of Advent and Christmas. Some include the whole liturgical year! You will find recipes, crafts, prayers, plays, background information, and more. Some of the sites are the work of one author, while other sites draw on the talents of many authors and include links to other web sites or blogs. Look for the words "Advent," "Christmas," or the saint's feast on the site to locate the material pertinent to your search.

www.catholiccuisine.blogspot.com

www.catholicculture.org

www.catholicholycards.org

www.catholicicing.com

www.cucinariodinonnaivana.blogspot.com (This blog is in Italian but has language translation capabilities.)

www.elizabethfoss.com *(in the heart of my home)*

http://familyfeastandferia.wordpress.com

http://foodsandfestivitiesofthechristianyear.blogspot.com

www.livingadvent.com

www.sjtb.org/releducolor.html

www.stnicholascenter.org

www.wf-f.org

BAKING:
COOKIE CUTTERS, MOLDS, AND CONVERSION TABLES FROM U.S. STANDARD TO METRIC BAKING

AMAZON.COM This popular online site sells Nativity Cookie Cutter Bake sets and Nativity Chocolate Molds year round, also Maple Leaf Molds. To view them go to **www.amazon.com**

CAKERECIPES-R-US Baking conversion tables **U.S. Standard to Metric** are offered on this site dedicated to "the largest collection of homemade cake recipes from scratch on the web." Be sure to check out their Christmas cake recipes! **http://www.cakerecipes-r-us.com/baking-conversions. html**

CATHOLIC CHILD A resource for nativity sets, Christmas cookie cutters, books and much more. To view their inventory: www.catholicchild.com or call for catalog 1-800-363-2233.

HOBI PICTURE COOKIE MOLDS Hand-carved St. Nicholas, angel molds and more by carver Gene Wilson. To view his inventory: **www.cookiemold.com** email:genewilson@cookiemold.com, or write: Hobi Cookie Molds, PO Box 25, Belleville, IL 62222-0025.

HOUSE ON THE HILL, INC. "Providing working replicas of historic cookie molds" for *Speculaas*, St. Nicholas, Christmas, and more. To view their inventory: **www.houseonthehill.net**, toll free: 877-279-4455 (U.S. only), phone: 630-279-4455, fax 630-279-5544. For a catalog email: support@houseonthehill, or write 650 West Grand Ave., Unit 110, Elmhurst, IL 60126.

KITCHEN KRAFTS They sell metal cookie cutter Nativity bake sets and plastic Nativity molds for chocolate, butter, wax and more. You can find them at **www.kitchenkrafts.com**

MORSE FARM MAPLE SUGAR WORKS, Family run maple sugar business in central Vermont since 1782. You will find a large line of maple sugar products, including maple sugar candy, **www. morsefarm.com** or 1-800-242-2740.

WILTON ENTERPRISES, INC. Large inventory of baking and decorating items may be viewed at **www.wilton.com.** Catalog available by email: **info@wilton.com,** or write Wilton Industries, 2240 W.75th St., Woodbridge, IL 60517, phone 630-963-1818 or 800-794-5866.

❧ LITURGICAL RESOURCES ☙

HOLY SEE The Vatican maintains a website which includes information on the liturgical year and the Holy Father's schedule. To view this site: **http://www.vatican.va**

UNITED STATES CONFERENCE OF CATHOLIC BISHOPS The bishops' national website contains a number of links to the liturgical calendar and catechetical materials that pertain to observing the seasons and feast days. Phone: 202-541-3000. To view this site: **www.usccb.org**

LITURGICAL CALENDARS for other English-speaking Catholics. Included are the web addresses for Australia, Canada, England & Wales, and Ireland. Click on each liturgical calendar to find saints' feast days unique to each country along with the feasts belonging to the General Roman Calendar for the Universal Church.

Australia: **http://www.catholic.org.au/**

Canada: nlo.cccb.ca/index.php/liturgical-calendar

England & Wales: **www.liturgyoffice.org.uk/calendar/index.shtm/**

Ireland: **www.catholicbishops.ie**

BIBLIOGRAPHY

Baggett, Nancy. *The International Cookie Cookbook*. New York: Stewart, Tabori & Chang, 1988.

Ball, Ann. *Catholic Traditions in Cooking*. Huntington, IN: Our Sunday Visitor Publishing, 1993.

———. *A Handbook of Catholic Sacramentals*. Huntington, IN: Our Sunday Visitor, 1991.

Barolini, Helen, *Festa: Recipes and Recollections of Italian Holidays*. Madison, WI: University of Wisconsin, 2002.

Berger, Florence. *Cooking for Christ: Your Kitchen Prayer Book*. National Catholic Rural Life Conference, 1949.

Bogle, Joanna. *A Book of Feasts and Seasons*. Herefordshire, UK: Fowler Wright Books, 1988.

Bradner, John. *Symbols of Church Seasons & Days*. Harrisburg, PA: Morehouse Publishing, 1977.

Braun, Terri, Jodi Evert, and Jeanne Thieme. *Kirsten's Cookbook: A Peek at Dining in the Past with Meals You Can Cook Today*. Middleton, WI: Pleasant Co., Publications, Inc., 1994.

Canon Law Society of Great Britain and Ireland. *The Code of Canon Law*. London, UK: Collins Liturgical Publications, 1983.

Carter, Susannah. *Frugal Housewife*. New York: G. & R. Waite, 1803.

Catholic Biblical Association of America. *The New American Bible*. New York: P. J. Kenedy & Sons, 1970.

Congregation for Divine Worship and Discipline of the Sacraments. *Directory of Popular Piet and the Liturgy*. Available at www.vatican.va/roman_curia/congregations/ccdds/ /documents/rc_con_ccdds_doc_20020513_vers-direttorio_en.html.

Congregation for Divine Worship. *Missale Romanum*, 2nd edition typica, "General Instruction of the Roman Missal," 1970. Promulgated by Pope Paul VI, 1st edition typica, 1969.

Ferguson, George. *Signs & Symbols in Christian Art*. London & New York: Oxford University Press, 1971.

Flannery, Austin, O.P., ed. *Vatican II Documents: The Conciliar and Post Conciliar Documents (New Revised Edition)*. Grand Rapids, MI: Wm. Eerdmans Publishing Co., 1992.

Giblin, James Cross. *The Truth About Santa Claus*. New York: Harpercollins, 1985.

Hardon, John, A., S.J. *The Catholic Catechism*. New York: Doubleday & Company, 1975.

———. *Modern Catholic Dictionary*. New York: Doubleday & Company, 1980.

Jeffers, H. Paul. *Legends of Santa Claus (A&E Biography)*. Minneapolis: Lerner Publications Co., 2001.

Johnson, Kevin, O. *Why Do Catholics Do That? A Guide to the Teachings and Practices of the Catholic Church*. New York: Ballantine Books, 1994.

Jones, Charles, W. *Saint Nicholas of Myra, Bari, and Manhattan*. Chicago & London: University of Chicago Press, 1978.

Kaufman, William, I. *The Catholic Cookbook: Traditional Feast and Fast Day Recipes*. New York: The Citadel Press, 1965.

Libreria Editrice Vaticana. *Catechism of the Catholic Church*, 2nd ed. Washington, DC: United States Catholic Conference, 1994, 2000.

Mathews, Wendell. *Basic Symbols and Terms of the Church*. Minneapolis: Fortress Press, 1971.

McGinley, Phyllis. *A Wreath of Christmas Legends*. New York: The MacMillan Co., 1967.

McLoughlin, Helen. *Family Advent Customs*. Collegeville, MN: The Liturgical Press, 1954.

———. *Family Christmas Customs*. Collegeville, MN: The Liturgical Press, 1956.

———. *My Nameday Come for Dessert*. Collegeville, MN: The Liturgical Press, 1962.

Nault, William, H., ed. *Christmas in the Netherlands*. Chicago: World Book Childcraft International, 1981.

Newland, Mary Reed. *The Year and Our Children*. San Diego: The Firefly Press, 1956.

Nissenberg, Sandra K., M.S.R.D. *The Everything Kids' Cookbook*. Adams, MA: Adams Media Corp., 2002.

Pope Paul VI. "Reflections at Nazareth." *The Pope Speaks* Vol. 9, no. 3 (1964).

Randall, Mary, *The Virginia Housewife*. Baltimore: Plaskitt & Fite, 1838.

Romero, José Leopoldo. *Betty Crocker's Mexican Cookbook*. New York: Random House, Inc., 1981.

Rooney, Colleen. "Saint Nicholas: Patron of Children is Making a Comeback." *Arlington Catholic Herald*, Arlington, VA. December 5, 1996.

Rundell, Maria Eliza. *A System of Domestic Cookery*. Boston, 1807.

Saunders, Rev. William, P. *Straight Answers*. Baltimore: Cathedral Foundation Press, 1998.

———. *Straight Answers II*. Baltimore: Cathedral Foundation Press, 1998.

Schuegraf, Ernst. *Cooking with the Saints*. San Francisco, Ignatius Press: 2001.

Sheraton, Mimi. *Visions of Sugarplums*. New York: Harper & Row, 1968, 1981.

Simmons, Amelia. *American Cookery*. Hartford, CT, 1798.

Thurston, Herbert, J., and Donald Attwater, eds. *Butler's Lives of the Saints*. Westminster, MD: Christian Classics, 1981.

United States Conference of Catholic Bishops. *The General Instruction of the Roman Missal*. Washington, DC: USCCB Communications, 2001.

Von Trapp, Maria. *Around the Year with the Trapp Family*. New York: Pantheon, 1955. Text available at http://www.ewtn.com/library/FAMILY/TRAPP/TXT.

Vitz, Evelyn, Birge. *A Continual Feast: A Cookbook to Celebrate the Joys of Family and Faith throughout the Christian Year*. San Francisco: Ignatius Press, 1991. First published 1985 by Harper & Row.

Weiser, Francis, S., S.J. *Handbook of Christian Feasts and Customs*. New York: Harcourt Brace and Company, 1952.

———. *The Christmas Book*. New York: Harcourt Brace and Company, 1952.

———. *The Holyday Book*. New York: Harcourt Brace and Company, 1956.

———. *Religious Customs*. Collegeville, MN: The Liturgical Press, 1956.

———. *The Year of the Lord in the Christian Home*. Collegeville, MN: The Liturgical Press, 1964.

COPYRIGHT ACKNOWLEDGMENTS

Made in the USA
Lexington, KY
09 November 2013